A PATH TO FREEDOM

A PATH TO FREEDOM

―――― EDITED BY ――――
LENARD D. MOORE
LeJUANE "EL'JA" BOWENS
SHANNON C. WARD

LONGLEAF PRESS
FAYETTEVILLE, NORTH CAROLINA

Longleaf Press
www.longleafpress.org

Copyright © 2024 by Longleaf Press.
All rights reserved.

Printed in the United States of America
ISBN: 9798988762430 (paperback)

Library of Congress Catalog Data:
Editors: Lenard D. Moore, LeJuane "El'Ja" Bowens, and Shannon C. Ward
Editorial Assistant: James Daniels
Title: A Path to Freedom: poems / anthology

Cover Art: "Sunset of my Last Living Brain Cell" by Roger Weingarten

TABLE OF CONTENTS

LENARD D. MOORE

Toward Healing i

MAUREEN ALSOP

Papaver Somniferum 1

Sweetwater Ardour 3

JOHN BALABAN

Soldier Home 4

Mr. Giai's Poem 5

Thoughts Before Dawn 7

Loving Graham Green 9

SAM BARBEE

Taxi-ing 11

Armed Forces 13

LEJUANE "EL'JA" BOWENS

A Soldier's Tale 15

SHANA BRUSHABER

Why I Served 18

Broken 19

ARLIN BUYERT

Dear Dad 20

Bone 21

Reunion 22

KELLIE CANNON

The Fragile Line 23

Burn It Down 24

On Fridays 26

The Aftermath 28

The Dog and You: Again 29

MELANIE COSTA

The Battle 31

DOUGLAS CROFT

Freedom 32

TOM DAVIS

The Three-Inch Cockroach 34

A Hungry Five Days 35

DEBORAH H. DOOLITTLE

Another Kind of Call and Response 36

The Morning of Your Deployment 37

Rain in Jacksonville 38

TIFFANI DENEEN FIELDS

Stay Humble 39

JANET FORD

My Father and I Have Nightmares 40

MICHAEL GAROFOLO

The Circle 42

JOHN GOSSLEE

My Beautiful Father the Fire Bird 43

Excerpt 45

SIREN HAND

The Time-Traveler's Suite 46

Birdwatching 54

EVA HELTON

Agent Orange! 56

MARY HENNESSEY

1967: Brooke Army Medical Center 57

Home to See My Brother 60

Avoidance and the Minotaur 62

VIRGINIA EWING HUDSON

Mean Business 64

ELIZABETH W. JACKSON

Soldier, Phoenix 66

LAVINIA JACKSON

United States Armed Forces 68

JACQUE JACOBS

The Last Official Face 71

ROLLIN JEWETT

What Did You Do in the War, Daddy? 72

MATTHEW JOHNSON

A Colored Regiment Returns from WWI 74

PAUL JONES

The Jumper 76

Testimony of J. Sidney Setzer (1841-1916) 77

MELISSA KELLEY

At What Cost 78

ANNE KISSEL

The Bombs Bursting in Air 79

CAROL KRAUSS

What Feeds the Wheat 81

RACHEL LANDSEE

Lullaby 82

Hold 84

BRENDA LEDFORD

Possum Byers 86

MARC LEVY

Casualty Poem 87

Eighteen Years After He Died 88

ROBERT LUNDAY

Fort Bragg 89

GABRIEL MARAVELAS

Recruit Poem 91

Rock My Boat 93

MARCHIANO

The Thing 94

LENARD D. MOORE

A Hum in the Living Room 96

Grandmother on the Porch 97

My Father Leaves for Vietnam 98

What Was Said on the Porch 99

Vietnam Haiku 100

ANDREW NEWBY

The Boys of Winter.. 101

KEITH OCKIMEY

The Struggle Is Real...103

I Feel Happy..105

CHARLES DANIEL PERRY "C.P. MAZE"

#MouthOfAMarine #MarineCorpMade.....................106

DAVID W. PLUNKETT

I Will Wear Sandals with Socks..............................109

BARBARA PRESNELL

Memorial Day, My Son Leaves Home 111

What Flutters 112

Planting the Garden 113

PAT RIVIERE-SEEL

Why Pronouns Matter 114

Firepower.. 115

GINA SINGLETON

    How Could I Not 116

    Dear Military Child 118

CINDY B. STEVENS

    Drip 120

    No Return War 122

LEE STOCKDALE

    Battlefield 124

GINA STREATY

    Black Stones 126

    A Letter Home 128

    Song: A Balm for the Decades 130

    Desert Storm 132

EDWARD SUPRANOWICZ

    The Skin of Things 134

RIC VANDETT

    The War 135

DANIEL WALTER

New Man 136

How the Shadow Hits Me 137

MICHAEL WHITE

Packed Away 139

TANYA WHITNEY

Only a Dream 141

What Can I Say 143

KATHERINE WOLFE

My Father's Gift 144

BOB WOOD

Father's hands 145

CONTRIBUTORS 146

ACKNOWLEDGMENTS 158

TOWARD HEALING

Here are fifty voices speaking toward healing. Not all the poets have seen the battlefield, though many of them have. Some of us served in the military during peacetime. Nonetheless, we have gone through the training and have lived on base and wore the uniform. We know the language. Yes, there certainly is military language, too. Many of us have grown up as military children. To that end, there are even generations of some of families who have served. In short, there is a brotherhood or familyhood of us. Like our blood kin, we military brothers and sisters are each other's keeper, too. In other words, we look out for each other. However, each one of us has lived a different story. So please witness our stories within these poems in this collection, *A Path to Freedom*. There are familiar voices, such as Maureen Alsop, John Balaban, Deborah H. Doolittle, Mary Hennessey, Paul Jones, Barbara Presnell, Pat Riviere-Seel, Gina Streaty, and Michael White within these pages. On the other hand, there are emerging voices, such as Kellie Cannon, Janet Ford, and Katherine Wolfe within these pages, too. We aim to feature Veterans or their family members with a connection to North Carolina here. For that reason, this collection of poems is not including the full spectrum of Veterans, meaning those who do not have the North Carolina experience. We have several bases in this state, such as Camp Lejeune, Fort Liberty (formerly Fort Bragg), Seymour Johnson Air Force Base, etc. We have schools, colleges and universities, which are military-friendly. We also have many businesses, which are military-friendly.

We hope that *A Path to Freedom* will enable readers to glean a deeper understanding of the tapestry of these varied stories from these lyrical voices. No one book can come close to the actual experiences, but maybe the sounds and sights through imagery and alliteration, assonance, consonance, onomatopoeia, repetition, and so forth, as well as metaphors and similes, can spark an awareness. We hope that our poems will transform you. We also hope that lessons could be learned from them. In addition, we hope that you will keep this book at your bedside, take it to parks, take it to beaches, take it to retreats, take it on road trips, take it on boats and ships, take it on airplanes, and share it with others. Then maybe the next collection of poems will depict love. What would the world be like with more love and less battles? We Veterans love to love, too. Because we're human, we're teeming with love. Because we're human, we don't want to leave our families for warfare. And yet, we certainly want freedom. If we spread the word about *A Path to Freedom,* then perhaps, these poems could make a difference. Let our voices resonate.

Again, here are fifty voices speaking toward healing. For healing, it is pertinent that we talk about and write about our military experiences and the impact on military children. Yes, military children have stories about their military parents. We must consider entire families.

I wonder whether or not one of these poets in *A Path to Freedom* will become the next Yusef Komunyakaa, the next Denise Levertov, the next Marilyn Nelson, or the next Brian Turner.

Lenard D. Moore,
Editor

Papaver Somniferum

Maureen Alsop

The trees dream a certain static. Summer is just
here. I dreamed I saw beauty. I dreamed you
lay at the road's edge. Or was it just the grass
in late sun. What toward me did you bring. This
meeting of one, my conspirator. We, of no
repercussion, lived once as the same body
                      I had always known
winter's sandhills at midpoint. Safety

is perception sometimes. Sometimes the signs
were not there. Restrictions grew. You woke, iron's
taste on the tongue, artillery smoke, your lips bled

mercy and thistle. First you used up hurt then
you gave away your neighbour.

It was an open equation, a
satisfaction....Your neighbour killed his neighbour. A
constellation in dispersion.

            Do what you may. And then again,
take the gun.

I held you in the field as the doctor
packed the wound. He said it was a stitch up. No
retribution came. It was simple

in unity to bind myself. There was no other
mark. Only this seam from another realm. Later, in the arbor,
under the eye of a tailorbird, the afternoon's

small apostate, I fell into renewal.

Sweetwater Ardour

Maureen Alsop

A stone fence you follow—
the same north lake

The snow waits on us

It is a good deep snow   And deep ash where
the beloved is not
forgotten

One where the war
is now
a softly glow
      softly, a move of air

the glow is beautiful here
beautiful
and mad

—the glow of the world

this one hour   love
lifts away

Soldier Home

John Balaban

*"At first Krebs ... did not want to talk about the war at all.
Later he felt the need to talk but no one wanted to hear about it."*
–Ernest Hemingway, "Soldier's Home"

Full moon over Beaufort Inlet, moon path
streaming towards him barefoot on the cold
beach, watching wave crests rush the shore.

Out in the Atlantic silence, boat lights wink
on a black horizon as a Camp Lejeune chopper
circles and circles a spot on the sea,

engine staccato louder than the waves, search
light beams brighter than the moon. Finally
it breaks off and heads landward,

just a wasp shape crossing the moon, cutting lights
at the shoreline, its engine loud in the boy's head.
Not even the waves can drown it.

"Captains and soldiers are smeared on the bushes and grass;
Our Generals schemed in vain," Li Po wrote, twelve hundred
years ago.

Mr. Giai's Poem

John Balaban

The French ships shelled Haiphong then took the port.
Mr. Giai was running down a road, mobilized
with two friends, looking for their unit in towns
where thatch and geese lay shattered on the roads
and smoke looped up from cratered yards. A swarm
of bullock carts and bicycles streamed against them
as trousered women strained with children, chickens,
charcoal, and rice towards Hanoi in the barrage lull.
Then, Giai said, they saw just stragglers.
Ahead, the horizon thumped with bombs.

At an empty inn they tried their luck
though the waiter said he'd nothing left.
"Just a coffee," said Mr. Giai. "A sip
of whisky," said one friend. "A cigarette," the other.
Miraculously, these each appeared. Serene,
they sat a while, then went to fight.
Giai wrote a poem about that pause for Ve Quoc Quan,
the Army paper. Critics found the piece bourgeois.

Forty years of combat now behind him
—Japanese, Americans, and French.
Wounded twice, deployed in jungles for nine years,
his son just killed in Cambodia,
Giai tells this tale to three Americans

each young enough to be his son:
an ex-Marine once rocketted in Hue,
an Army grunt, mortared at Bong Son,
a C.O. hit by a stray of shrapnel,

all four now silent in the floating restaurant
rocking on moorlines in the Saigon river.
Crabshells and beer bottles litter their table.
A rat runs a rafter overhead. A wave slaps by.
"That moment," Giai adds, "was a little like now."
They raise their glasses to the river's amber light,
all four as quiet as if carved in ivory.

Thoughts Before Dawn

—for Mary Bui Thi Khuy, 1944-1969

John Balaban

The bare oaks rock and snowcrust tumbles down.
The creaking eave woke me thinking of you
crushed by a truck decades ago
when the drunk soldier lost the wheel.

We brought to better care the nearly lost,
the boy burned by white phosphorus, chin
glued to his chest; the scalped girl;
the triple amputee from the road-mined bus;
the kid without a jaw; the one with no nose.
You never wept in front of them, but waited
until the gurney rolled them into surgery.
I guess that's what amazed me most.
Why didn't you fall apart or quit?

Once, we flew two patched kids home,
getting in by Army chopper,
a Huey Black Cat that skimmed the sea.
When the gunner opened up on a whale
you closed your eyes and covered your ears
and your small body shook in your silk *ao dai*.
Oh, Mary. In this arctic night, I lie in my bed
and rehearse your smile, bright white teeth,

the funny way you rode your Honda 50: perched
so straight, silky hair bunned up in a brim hat,
front brim blown back, and dark glasses.
Brave woman, I hope you never saw the truck.

Loving Graham Green
—*for Gloria Emerson*

John Balaban

"But in Indo-China I drained a magic potion, a loving-cup which I have shared since with many retired colon *and officers of the Foreign Legion whose eyes light up at the mention of Saigon and Hanoi." -Graham Greene, Introduction,* The Quiet American.

So there he was, decades after the war,
rattled and adrift, waiting in the waiting room of a shrink in
New Mexico, of all places,

an office in a garden by an adobe house its tin roof
aflame with sunlight
as the sun humped across blue sky

and hummingbirds raced to plunder heads
of purple cosmos and bee balm while sunflowers looked up like a
congregation seeking benediction.

Beyond the garden, the river surged over canyon rocks
and piñon snags where big trout lurked in the cold
shadows of dark pools.

He was on vacation; he hadn't planned this visit. The wife and
kids were taking the trail ride.
He had found the name in the phone book.

After a lot of babble and blubbering, the guy asked him if
he knew what was wrong,
what was hurting him so, why he was crying,

why he was here. He shook his head
"no." No,
he didn't know.

"Still a reporter?" Yes. "Successful?" Yes, pretty
much. "Happily married?" Well, yeah.

"But your eyes," he said, "are dead, except when
you mention Vietnam and then a little spurt of
epinephrine

zings your system and your eyes light up." The therapist
charged sixty bucks, suggested he take up skydiving.

*Driving back to the riddled heap of villagers
from which someone had pulled out a live 3-year old,
past the berm-wire where they were still yanking off*

*the bodies, he was flying in a chopper when it dove down to open up on a
lone elephant in a field of sugar cane.
After a gin fizz on the veranda of the Continental Palace,*

he was back at the motel where everyone was by the pool,
the kids all lit up after their trail ride high on the canyon rim,
where the air was sweet with pine and bear grass, the sky clear.

Taxi-ing

Sam Barbee

Downtown rain is cold rain.
On a moonless night, the city's
precise edges acquire a frosty blur.
Beneath blue neon, the weary taunt themselves
with memos and rote movement. Dreaming
of short money, the homeless and illegitimate
scavenge dry butts.
                     Midnight - the rain stiffens.
Locked temples and tabernacles brood.
I wait at an empty corner.
From inside a bus, a choir of parents
peer down at me. I fumble for my case
and umbrella. Bus-riding provokes me.

        i imagine myself inside the bus:
        old men waiting, watching each rivulet
        of rain drip from my sleeve.
        clasped into plaid overcoats
        women permit plastic shopping bags
        to encroach in the aisle
        like poorly-raised children.

I hail a splashing taxi - its refuge:
wide vinyl seats and riskless peace.
A Iraq survivor grips the wheel.
Like a paraplegic, only his neck rolls.
                     "Just Drive."

He nods and meters a one-syllable world.
I close the door on the day,
on all that cowers in the rain.
Downtown rain is silent rain.

                    We shimmer
down a shining street. From his mirror,
my steward wants destinations. Perhaps
to the countryside - away from the leash
and the wretched trees.

          there is a pasture, clover wet with dew.
          lavender morning glory laces white fences.
          ripe fruit waits on a table. an old man
          wears a checked shirt, his soft hands

Armed Forces

Sam Barbee

NBC blared, "Kennedy is dead."
I was out of school: Thanksgiving Holidays—
turkey legs and stuffing—
not much traffic—not the usual neighbors walking.
My dad sat on the back steps, and
worked up enough saliva to expel a bloody paste
onto the ground. *Curse this hurt.*
The dentist had yanked his final incisors.

All his teeth had withered from suffering fevers
from malaria and diphtheria in North Africa.
You know, the President was a veteran,
just like me. Both battlin' that Axis.
He had hard evidence: black and white snapshots
of pyramids—the Sphinx—bare-breasted native girls—
elephants—Staff Sergeant of the motor pool
that drove Rommel from the dunes—the Victory Story.

I hope they hang that son-of-a-bitch. Then,
he motioned for me to come close. *Son, little fellas*
shouldn't say grown-up words like that. Okay?
I nodded and hugged him. His body stiffened.
You're a good boy. . . . I just hope
that'll be enough. Curse this hurt. . . .
His stale cigarette breath made me gasp. He spit again,
bloody paste curdling in dust. *Curse this hurt.*

That night snug in bed, the television still buzzed.
My lips silently formed the new phrase:
son-of-a-bitch
into the wrinkles of my white pillow.

A Soldier's Tale
—*based off of A Soldier's Story*

LeJuane "El'Ja" Bowens

Here I go again
Writing about my time in war again
The ongoing struggle of trying not to relive
The battles I've had to fight
Outside…and in

But isn't this what makes for good drama
The grizzled veteran who gathers up people
To peel back the bandages around them
And share their war wounds as war stories

I wonder if you believe me
If I told you that this was, and still is an endless paradox
Knowing that no matter where you go
Shit like this still follows me around like a shadow

To be a veteran
Is to be a hero
To be a black veteran
Is to be a hero
Until the country's ready to vilify you

But to be a black veteran who's hated by your own
Well, that's where it gets tricky
It becomes a riddle
Better yet, a joke

I mean you find yourself fighting for rights to be equal
And to some degree it works
Because equality comes
When racism don't let you forget your past
While black don't let you forget racism build America as a barrel
And turned us into the crabs trying to out of it

No idea is original under the sun
Not even the idea to work for something greater
That is until Racism hides behind Patriotism
While Internalized Racism have you hating your own people
And claim that you're doing it for the culture

Master SGT Waters is a pure example of this conundrum
A Black veteran that despised racism
But despised black people even more if they didn't fit his perception
Of what we should be

So much so, it drove C.J. Memphis to suicide
A veteran that wanted to do nothing more but enjoy the world
But ultimately paid the price with his life
When Master SGT Waters stated the Black Race
Couldn't afford him anymore

I feel the noose around my neck
Every time I feel like I am closer to feeling this plight
A veteran at odds with a country that don't want me here
But thanks me for my service because they have the freedom to tell me that

And also a black man
Who sometimes feel like what things I may say or do
Would have me on the outside of my race looking in
Because proper etiquette seems like white mannerisms

This is a fence I have to straddle daily
And it hurts
But then, we know the story of the soldier
We suck it up and drive on

However,
There are times I feel like I'm walking a tightrope
Stuck in the middle of what side to proceed to

But as C.J. Memphis stated
"Any man ain't sure where he belong,
gotta' be in a whole lotta pain."

Why I Served

Shana Brushaber

You want to know the reason why I served? I served, because I love my country. If I could go back and do it all over again I would. Integrity first, service before self, and excellence in all we do.

Why did I serve? I served, because I love my country. I reported my sexual assault, and I faced retaliation. I was isolated from my peers, and then betrayed by my peers. I served, because I love my country.

I was made fun of. I was disrespected. I cleaned the toilets and mopped the floors. I also cleaned up the office. I am going to let you know why I served. I served, because I love my country.

I was put on the do-not-arm list, and I was committed to the psych ward three times: twice for suicide ideation, and once for homicide ideation. Why did I serve? I am going to let you know why I served. I served, because I love my country.

They ruled my case he said she said. They believed he misunderstood the word no. I was discharged for adjustment disorder. If I had the chance to do it all over again, I would. Even though I know the outcome, I would still do it over again. Why would I do it over again? Because I am proud to have served the country I love.

BROKEN

Shana Brushaber

You broke me. Are you happy now? I will never be me again Before I took an oath, I was fearless, full of life, did whatever I wanted, didn't give a fuck about the consequences. I was unstoppable

After I took the oath, I felt safe. I was respected. I was worthy. I became more fearless, well organized. I had a brighter future. I finally realized there were consequences for my actions.

Now, I'm broken, shattered into millions of pieces, impossible to be put back together again, betrayed by the same person, that took the same oath.

Now, I am fearful, no longer feel hopeful, no longer have a future. I'm no longer worthy. You broke me. Are you happy now? I will never be the same again.

The country that I once loved is now the country I fear. I no longer feel safe, shattered into a million piece I will never be able to be put back together again. I will never be the same person I once was. Are you happy now?

I am broken…forever

Dear Dad

Arlin Buyert

Dear Dad

December 11, 1968
Da Nang

Not sure how to write this letter.
I feel far away from the farm—
front pasture, Rock Creek,
garden, windmill, Grandpa,
far from church and Sunday school class,
so far from you and Mom.

Here, I'm also removed—
from my killing.
I guess it's best that way.
I drop bombs from 10,000 feet,
scurry back to the carrier
to look at reconnaissance photos
of the village I destroyed,
where, they said, "no women or children,"
only to drink and play poker into the night.
Then again, tomorrow.

It's not like I figured. Please
don't tell Mom too much.

Love, your son.

BONE

Arlin Buyert

Oh the load we carried
home from 'Nam.
The general ordered
"kill the damn enemy,
every one of them."

But the woman,
scarf wrapped around her head,
waist deep in a swamp,
young son wearing a bamboo hat
nestled in her arms.

Now I hear the chopper,
taste sweat on my lips,
smell blood in the dirt,
see bone on the road
as I walk my children to school.

REUNION

Arlin Buyert

Ten thousand white grave markers,
aligned on the high bluff
far above the now quiet Normandy Beach,
I see a father and son embrace,
for a long time, at one of them.

The Fragile Line

Kellie Cannon

the one that starts at the edge
of the porcelain plate, the
ceramic mug, as thin as
a strand of hair,
and the slightest bump
bursts it further, ice cracking
on the pond, stretching
like spider veins on a thigh
or rather like cracks
in a hidden molar that
does the daily work
of eating, clenching,
keeping you quiet or silent
and all at once
you feel it
shooting down, into roots
and hidden nerves
and that is when
the line has gone too far
too deep to know
you are the one
who can't control
the response,
the fight or flight
of life or your love
rolling over in bed
as you say a silent
goodnight.

Burn It Down

Kellie Cannon

The blaze ahead in the caravan was not yours but true fire
scars your eyes. You carry something now—through fire.

You do not come home alone. There is war in your body
and mind. Alone, I'm never on this journey where you fire

shots at the enemy, where you keep the loaded gun
with you, closer than any desire you want to pursue. Fire

empty glares out the windshield where you stay on track,
in tracks, following tracks to avoid undue fire;

where Humvees explode into particles of junk and ash in the sky
with nothing left in you but fear and anger to ensue fire

until you are alone in your thoughts, again, sleeping
in Kevlar to protect you from new fire,

and the danger that exists in your head, your body,
the one that abandons you in the night blue. Fire.

The cot never could hold the weight of your body,
couldn't cradle your flesh and pain, too. Fire

lights inside, finds the parts of your being
no one and nothing can touch, places to brew fire—

No, Kellie, it's not your flame to smother.
He's yours to love; it's his to starve. Take your cue, Fire.

On Fridays

Kellie Cannon

We wear red
to remember
everyone deployed,
their losses,
        your losses,
        our losses,
the losses we have not yet faced,
the ones in the middle of the night,
in the organic aisle of Big Y,
in the endless loop
of rooms at Ikea,
in the labyrinth of stones at
that park we can never remember the name of
but you can name the color of the grass
and I can name the peace
I search for,
in the crowd of patriots
waiting for the fireworks
to explode
over a high school
neither of us attended,
        in the tic of your fingers
grasping at something
when nothing is there,
in the incessant beeping
of the kitchen fire alarm
because I didn't clean the stove again,

       because you didn't say sorry
            again
       because I am not sorry
         I am sorry
because I know you are
         again,
in the corner of your mouth
where you bite your whiskers—
the overgrown, the white, the red—
in the parking lot
of Diana's Bathe
where the spots are full
and we need to leave soon
but we are both
empty.

The Aftermath

Kellie Cannon

His elbow brushes the base of the fork,
sweeping it off the table into the air.

The fork twirls, spiraling until it reaches
the ground. The polished silver catches his eye

as he stares like he sees something familiar
and horrifying—like the words in sentences

he stops in mid-thought, or the flashes
that would wake him each night as he slept

in Kandahar. Minutes later,
he remains still. He doesn't bend to grab the fork;

instead, he raises his eyes to the ceiling,
willing to taste nothing except air

beating into his mouth from the ceiling fan.
I imagine it all tastes strange to him,

familiar but gone because
we are both relearning things.

I crouch down and get his fork.
I'll deal with the cleaning later.

The Dog and You: Again

Kellie Cannon

He whimpers beside me
in the dead of night.
I grab the phone – 12:30.
I reach out and touch him,
rub behind his ears,
confused why he is shoving
his muzzle under my arm.

Then, boom.
An explosion of purple
presents itself in the sky
outside our bedroom window.
In slow motion, the firework dances down
like glitter from a canister.
He shakes and forces his front paws
onto the bed. I invite him in
and lift his tired legs.
Age always shows first in the body.

He hasn't jumped into bed in years.
You call him and tap the middle of bed
and cover him in comfort
with your weighted blanket.
His heartbeat slows,
and his eyes feel

the weight of night
again. And me,
I don't know why
I don't cover you
with my weight,
my calm. And you,

you are gone again;
back into the war.
You are running away
again.
I know you'll return;
you always do,
but something is always gone,
always again.

The Battle

Melanie Costa

We were at war, supposed to have each other back. Never did I think the enemy would be one of my own.

With no disregard or remorse, you took my trust, innocence, and self-worth in seconds.

You walked away like I was nothing, leaving me with three choices; one, shoot you, act like it didn't happen, or kill myself.

I chose to act like it didn't happen to survive the war by numbing my emotions even more than before.

Then, I came home, it all came rushing back, and I needed to numb my brain.

Now, I'm learning, realizing it wasn't my fault, and you are to blame.

You took advantage of the situation, and there was nothing I could do to stop it.

You no longer have power, I have overcome, and I stand here a powerful woman for the battle I have won.

Freedom

Douglas Croft

I raised my hand
Took a stand
Fought for my country
And freedom in this land

I humped the boonies
Tunnels I did crawl
Faced the enemy terror
Bravely without stall

I flew that sortie
Dropped those targeted bombs
I reconned the aftermath
Cheered with military song

I cleared those buildings
Followed my orders
Bravely snuck
Behind enemy borders

I dodged bullets
And shot a few
I took men's lives
Protecting all of you

I saw friends die
From evil's unflinching hate
Daily considered
What might be my fate

I walked the line
In freedom's defense
Saw friends die
Freedom's expense

I'll not tell anymore
It is hard to describe
Am proud to have served
Thrilled to make it out alive

Home now
Not sure where to turn
Sometimes scream in the night
Sometimes my stomach churns

How long will it take
'Til I stop fighting this war
How long will it be
To know what for

I love my spouse
My family too
They try to understand
My journey isn't through

The Three-Inch Cockroach

Tom Davis

Since most of the Teamhouse was underground
or behind layers of sandbags, it was humid
and filled with bugs. On my first night,
I lay awake in my boxer shorts enduring
the oppressive heat and humidity,
trying to get to sleep when something
ran across my back. I jumped out of bed
and grabbed my flashlight just in time
to see a three-inch cockroach scuttle into the shadows.
Eventually, I got used to sharing my bed with these
and other creatures. It worked fine as long as they
didn't stop when they crossed my back or legs.

A Hungry Five Days

Tom Davis

On my first operation, the Team Leader handed me
several cans of mackerel packed in tomato sauce,
telling me how great they were.
I had packed my ruck sack with
Principal Indigenous Rations (PIRs),
the green tinfoil bags of dried food
that we provided the CIDG for field operations.
For that operation I had packed fish, squid, and pork packages.
When we stopped at noon for "pok time"
I opened a can of mackerel and took a bite.
God, it tasted like slimy raw fish.
About the only thing I could eat was rice from the PIRs.
It was a hungry five days for me.

Another Kind of Call and Response

Deborah H. Doolittle

I am running in the park at dawn
with bird songs accompanying
my every step, the cardinals
in the hedges, the mocker from
atop that tree, and the jays crying
to each other in the distant pines,
when I hear coming to me from
across the New River, Marines
shouting out as they run, much like
these birds. One of them calls out
the cadence, one or two words
reduced to vowel sounds, and
the others respond with different
sounds. Together, they keep a rhythm
my feet make as I round the paved
walkways in the park. They could be
lined up, in formation, running
in skivvies or in boots with full
combat gear. They could be doing
early morning calisthenics,
jumping jacks and burpees, for all
I know. I cannot see them and
the words I hear are not very
clear. It's not like I've seen that scene
a million times before. A slight
exaggeration, I know.
Together, we pound that unforgiving
pavement at the start of each day.

The Morning of Your Deployment

Deborah H. Doolittle

And I am down on my knees,
weeping, sweeping the detritus

we called living clean away.
If there is such a thing as

immaculate then this kitchen
comes close. You, who by now sit

belted inside the belly
of a transport plane, your gear

and sea bag secured, must just
imagine this conception.

Me, down on my knees, scrubbing
the linoleum, dragging

the bucket of suds behind
me like a ball and chain, claim

these stains—coffee, milk, blood, wine—
the enemy. There's no retreat,

no hurry, just this constant
worry I can't quite wipe clean

away before the children
wake, to begin each day this way.

Rain in Jacksonville

Deborah H. Doolittle

floods the streets like a stopped up
tub, like the proverbial flood
Noah's ark was meant for.

Yet drivers plow right on through
the deluge, making waves,
making mistakes in judgment.

Learning the meaning of hydro-
plane. Not misty, moisty wisps
of rain, but drops that pack a wallop,

clog drains, fog brains, bog down
the pace of traffic in the fast
lane. For ten solid minutes,

or half an hour, we all become
Marine-based amphibians,
slogging around Camp Lejeune.

Stay Humble

Tiffani Deneen Fields

Strengthened. United by story.
Transparent in pain.
Authentic in identity.
You give Light.

Honor to share and serve.
Unity in passion, drive, purpose.
Moved to action.
Bold but scared. Scarred.
Legacy of Healing birthed.
Empower the Future Others.

My Father and I Have Nightmares

Janet Ford

I see you Father
when the snakes came
green under the covers.
They came damp

palms over
my twelve-year-old
thighs with open
mouths

while just across the sheetrock
that barn in France
burned to the ground again
on your watch.

There's the slippered scuff
of your tartan flannels,
dowdy and warm
with the smell of the bed;

your soldier's eyes,
methadoned and mild.
A simple thing,
the comfort of a child.

How does the world come to be
out of nothing?
You hold out your Eveready;
light strafes the mystery.

Chin-stubble wattles
in uplight –
this face
has known the enemy.

Now the gnarls
of your broken hands
take the corners of my sheet
and the night air snaps

like laundry on a line
as white wings rise;
I feel the flap of a bird
trapped in my bed.

Fly! You said things
only I could hear.
I bellow strength
to climb the air

and when I let go
the bedsheet falls like sleep.
I still see
how it slews

and banks
across the brightening
to land at last, my Father,
at your feet.

The Circle

Michael Garofolo

Hello. Goodbye.
Gone in an instant, the blink of an eye.
Where did it go?
The life. The time.
It started with Hello.

My Beautiful Father the Fire Bird

John Gosslee

Today is the day of finishing little tasks.

The words of his body locked in a stroke
the doctors can't edit.

*

He walks through the brown
field in Vietnam, the ambush,
the Agent Orange pedals in his sweat.

The nurse spoons in pureed beets,
wipes his mouth, elevates the dead
hand that was filled with fire.

*

He held my wings in one
hand, the scissors in the
other
and after the clip I beat my
wings so much harder to fly.

He steers my face's pale fire
from the psychiatrist to the
hospital, the stomach pump, the
in-patient.

He says,
*whoever you become
now, I will love him.*

*

And father, people have begun
to love my words, chewed so
hard in your mouth, dropped
into mine.

Excerpt

John Gosslee

In the desert, clouds disappear and the sky goes on.
The football game broadcast doesn't replay
the width of her cinnamon temple
against my chapped lips.

The orange slice tastes like a leather bag full of stale water,
but I've missed the sweet for so long,
my body is one big taste bud
and I'm spitting seeds in a jar,
wishing everything was like it was before.

Her hips one bird chasing the other.
She scratches my back and rubs my shaved scalp,
the future is under my feet like a concrete floor.

The Time-Traveler's Suite

Siren Hand

Movement I: A black hole is a place in space where gravity pulls so much that even light cannot get out. (science.NASA.gov)

1986 - When I was younger, I swore
the adults were making *black holes* up,
some boogeyman to behave for:

get yourself right, otherwise
(faster than a blink)
everything you've known could fold in on itself;

you'll be smooshed by gravity – *SPLAT!*
Everything jammed together so tight
your skin and your brother's skin will be *touching*.

                                          Is there any worse punishment?

2022 - Yes. You are lemon-pressed mishmash & hodgepodge
collage of movie tickets, funeral flyers, protests:
the lovemaking and violence that connects them all.

Yes: You are stonebaked clay relay
beached in homegrown conversations,
both the ones that happened and the ones you can't get over.

Yes. At one point you were not here;
at another, you won't be again.

>Will they know to look for you?
>>Will they moondust for your fingerprints?

Yes. You are every folded possibility
and your home becomes your destination -and- departure point;
>your family is strange -and- strangers.
You are folded into everything you could have been,
crushed beyond moving to make things worse

like in 2011: I smooshed the spider in the shower
and realized (faster than a blink)
that fear must have felt like a black hole.

Movement II: Falling through an event horizon is literally passing beyond the veil — once someone falls past it, nobody could ever send a message back. They'd be ripped to pieces by the enormous gravity.
(Dr. Richard Massey - Institute for Computational Cosmology at Durham University)

First try:
I love you. I love you so much, I will join an army for you, and we can get married, and you can have healthcare, and we can try, start a family the *right way* this time and I can travel to a place not Bremerhaven, Fort Sill or Monterey, not Minsk or Moscow or Garmisch or DC (again). We can write distanced love letters like they did in Vietnam and World War II. I can vow to come back when I eventually realize my body is too old for this shit, but not for kissing you. We can have a houseboat, maybe in Guam, sip on pina coladas or whatever they drink there until we are married for three years and I see you for fifty-six days of it, until we realize that I'd never come back—

even if I wanted to.

Second try:
I love you so much, I am in stupid Texas feeling my skin boil off the bone. I have never wanted to be here in my whole life, especially with the stupid Army, hundreds of miles of prairie to ruck through to get buried in. So, you're welcome to that, and whatever else I have; and you're welcome to travel and meet my family (like I met yours) while I do this stupid training with this stupid base and wilted DFAC salad. All I ask is you trust me: I'm a world away I'm thinking of you because you're the only thing that'll make it any good. I'll change my name to yours if you stick around.

How do you make someone you love believe you?

Third Try.
I love you so much. I would tell you more, but nothing I say will keep you here.

                                                                 Yes: like that.

Movement III: The Shuttle Test Director performs the traditional call to stations and the countdown clock is activated.
(NASA – Countdown 101)

10. After this, there would be nothing
folded into itself
so I will stay for now.

9. My last breath
would still sustain
a newborn's first.

8. The sharpness of premature birth
grips the lifeline of my palms
with its nails—

7. I awe microscopic at his fingerprints,
watch the labyrinths grow to scat free flow scripture,
worship grain wave and moon phase alike.

6. I pray that he be/come
justified & protected in his truth, cradled
in reeds of river basket or pan flute

5. basking in the revolution's
clock hands, suns and planets.

4. I am wood owl, blind & starry eyed
with a map to the universe I can't see
or account for

3. but I will be here for as long as it takes
to sing your safety into the wind.

2. I am closed eyes, backwards-counting
marco poloing to the ashes & dust
that became and become us.

1. So I will stay for now:
After this, there would be nothing
folded into itself—

0. the shape of a full circle.

Movement IV: "For this reason, black holes are considered an edge of space, a one-way exit door from our universe; nothing inside a black hole can ever communicate with our universe again, even in principle. (Harvard Smithsonian Center for Astrophysics)

FROM THE TIME TRAVELLER:
I know you've been waiting
to hear from me. I promise:
I'm still here, but there's something
you should know.

        These transmissions,
        they only last so long.

                The last time, I needed
                to get a message across
                time & space
                IT

was maybe a little

        disrupt
ed but

      I still tried andwhenIdid
      it just screwed up everything

                maybe because
                I told you
                (You, me. Whatever):

      something I shouldn't have,
      or maybe just

LOOK- I'm running out of time
    this is so im

        port

            ant to your trajectory:

You can't come back. / Even if you wanted to / but this will change your
life/ love/ relationship/ family/ career/ passion project/ experiment/ outcome
ItWillMakeEverythingYou'veBeenThroughWorthItIPromiseIPromiseIProm
You've been eating Hope for so long: this is the feast of it. You are

            END OF TRANSMISSION

Birdwatching

Siren Hand

Morning coffee as normal.
I divide my front window into tic-tac-toe grid,
nine-section phone keypad.
It's easier for me that way,
to map how the birds come and go
free-form patterns of flight.

Take this, the case study–
At 11:37 (Local time):
    one adult male sparrow darts
    from Northwest Field of View (Keypad 1)
    to sundeck feeder (Keypad 5), squabbles with
    two already-present adult male
    sparrows. Two female juncos and two starlings squabble
    over seed. They peck at each other for greeting,
    establish status, take freely from what's allowed.

Also 1218 (Local): All of them dig
    at the ground in Keypad 8, scramble
    for the yield of another's destruction.
    Seed spills from the feeder (Keypad 5 to Keypad 8).

At 1334L:
    one military-aged male
–no, sorry, correction–
    one adult male cowbird glides
    from SE FOV to ground food at KP8.

At 1345L: one adult male sparrow departs
    from KP5 to KP3, out of NE FOV.
1346L-1400L: their activity continues,
    Nothing Significant to Report.
1143L: my dog blitzes, tumbles
    in froth-mouthed uninvited explosion,
    deepest joy at sunlight-scattered colors–
    no soul left in aftershock.

How long does one watch after the upset,
wait for destruction reset
for no trace, no next pattern—
for life to return to normal?
If I wait, or watch, perhaps
I'll see Bright Boy—
        slim cardinal, not yet witness to how
        his body will shimmer,
will scatter in the sun,
will form both fountain and firework.

I divide my front window into nine-section,
It's easier for me that way, to sit
Still / watching / waiting / wondering
if they'll all ever come back.

AGENT ORANGE!
—for Levi Helton

Eva Helton

Agent Orange!
Skull & Crossbones!
Aptly put!
Poison!
Johnson made it *Hush, Hush.*
Thought he wouldn't get caught!
It got in our DNA.
Caused problems in our kids for generations.
Learning disabilities, heart defects, diabetes,
Spinal bifida, cleft lips and palates, other defects too hard to mention.
Miscarriages in our wives, heartbreaks.
Then, later in us,
Cancers!
Pancreatic, Prostate, Skin, Leukemia,
Parkinson's, Diabetes,
You name it!
Late casualties!
Poison!
We are dying of it!
Many before the VA recognizes or compensates it!
All because Johnson, *Hush, Hushed* it!

1967: Brooke Army Medical Center

Mary Hennessey

Wagner and chopper blades
in the apocalypse by Coppola—
the Second Coming and it ain't Jesus.
In another version, Janis Joplin throws back
a long swallow of Southern Comfort
and hums the chorus of Bobby McGee
while round-eyed women move,
as if underwater,
in the dreams of leftover boys.

Around the dressing cart,
a quartet of the wounded, silly and raucous with relief—
the dirt of Southeast Asia still between their toes—
sings along with Grace Slick:
Don't you want somebody to love?
The nurse, perfume in the hem of her uniform,
and assigned to dressings for the duration,
tears tape and shifts packages of sterile gauze.

Flying overhead, chopper pilots ride manhole covers—
jury-rigged beneath them, as armor
for the underbelly of the bird
and drop boys from Nebraska and the neighborhood
into the story-high poinsettias of San Antonio.
Stateside—
who could have believed it—?

Near the quadrangle,
in the orthopedic and amputee wards,
a wound in every bed—
those who can—
race wheelchairs down hospital ramps at speeds
no longer possible on foot and hitch
rides downtown in their blue convalescent pajamas,
where in bars decorated with Christmas lights in March,
older men, with limbs still attached,
talk Texas
and buy them drinks,
until the MPs pick them up by the scruffs of their necks,
like so many half-drowned kittens
and bring them back to the ward.

Lieutenant, are these yours?

Those who cannot—
eat pizza from the wagon that moves
through the ward like the seasons
and in that claustrophobic space stockpile pain
pills for a boy from Louisiana
who will need them.

From beds, strung with aluminum chains
of the flip tops from empty beer cans,
other patients, lined up like children in a pew on Sunday morning,
negotiate the business of love with whores
and flirt with nurses—
the women
who work the floor in metered waves.

Hey lieutenant, want to feel my new leg?

A boy from Carolina—
really, they were just boys—
after two tours as a medic,
without pleasure in the ramp races or the women,
tries to hurl himself through the 4th floor window.
He cannot see the bars.
The wardmaster, an ex-middleweight from Chicago,
carries the boy away.

A 70-year-old Red Cross volunteer—
near that same window and slowed by the memory—
moves like the young women in their dreams.
She holds a clutch of mail for bedside delivery in one hand
and offers of matrimony in the other—
her would-be-lovers, boys the age of her grandchildren.
Later that day, the Green Bay Packers win the Super Bowl
and Silver Stars and Purple Hearts,
out of their red plush boxes,
whirl between the orthopedic-framed beds
like chopper blades or comets,
bright and brief.

Home to See My Brother

Mary Hennessey

Francis, you, all unanswered questions look like a poem to me.

Driving west and startled by
the measure of sky—
the telephone lines beaded with dark birds.

The landscape rolls over, exposes
shelves of stone, uncut pasture grasses.
During military leaves and Vietnam

we drank Texas Rum and Coke
at the Red Onion on Broadway. Sat outside
on the curb and sang, *If it takes forever....*

In high school, you painted *Help* in white paint
on the roof
outside your bedroom window.

You entered the Christian Brothers after graduation.
Logan Crosky, Kansas City's chief of police
called mama to be sure you were gone.

Francis, you, all unanswered questions look like a poem to me.

In the convalescent center a woman
in the hallway cries because she can't find her room.
The nurse pours fluids into a rubber tube

in your belly and we hold hands (yours unfamiliar
in this institutional light)
and sing the only song we know.

At the window a cloud of birds lifts as one—
held together by its own surface tension—
an unseen and elementary binding of one

small dark bird to another.
My brother, war-ruined 40 years ago, is dying and I wonder:
What is it about the winter grass that breaks the heart?

Avoidance and the Minotaur

Mary Hennessey

The winter light strung out
from pole to telephone pole
trips a sparrow in mid-flight.

The paper boy's car
a low flying plane
his headlight hits

the window's river-glass
then sheets like water.
No newspaper this morning, please

the dead from yesterday's pile up
like laundry.
In every room women

keen and count syllables
in old poems
trying to make something add up.

In the end what saves us
are the crossword puzzles,
reading Dickinson

past wild grasses
roseate, flattened,
pinned beneath pitch clouds—

seldom looking up
from careful pages
to see where we are going

to see anything at all
and wondering
how we got here so quickly.

Dickinson's slant truth
the intervening light
draws us along—

the thread
in the many-tongued maze
a consolation.

Mean Business

Virginia Ewing Hudson

The arroyo wrinkles behind me
I hold Cipriano's M-16 assault rifle
Wind blows my hair

Soft clouds dot the wide open sky
I don't like guns
Sunglasses may hide this, but

I wouldn't have said no anyway
I want to understand this gentle person
Front-lined at eighteen

Forced to witness and perpetrate horrors
Left to contemplate these formative events
Through years of nightmares

Shifting psychic landscapes
Guns his link to then and now
As he fires deep into the arroyo

First the weapons used by one side
Then those of the other
The ones used against him

Firing low that nothing might fly
Over the next mesa
To injure an innocent beyond

You hold it, he bids me
Let me take your picture
I, who have mostly held a cello and bow

You hold it
Now look tough
Look like you mean business

Soldier, Phoenix

Elizabeth W. Jackson

His mind is a desert; it's winter
        and he drives a road that's endless.
His buddy's body, a desecration

blasted into parts
        he can't reassemble—
the hand and forearm he wrestled

to the table one night, the arm
        that muscled up
for a second round-- no more

than meat. There is no phoenix,
        only scorching sand, refracted light,
and helicopters that ascend

with the mangled and dead.
        He must live with the lift
of acceleration, his boat's pound-and-bounce

and his daughter pushing herself up
        colt-legged on skis.
His hound, however arthritic,

still rocks up to all fours,
        and there's his own body
jerking upright rinsed in sweat

from the explosion of dreams.
        Empty beer cans.
Coffee, mug after mug.

He studies the twists of vapor
        before tossing down the final bite
of black silt. He has few desires

beyond the call of metal and machines.
        His arms tingle and itch
for that place deep in the belly

of his Mustang's engine—
        the '68 crankshaft, pistons, brake drum,
each smooth and rounded as a gun's barrel.

United States Armed Forces

Lavinia Jackson

United
Armed Forces
Make statements
Under
Huge
tattered rectangles
halfway round the world
Proclaiming places
Glassy distances
With uninvited invasion
Stating
Defense is
Arbitrary map lines tethered
To trees older than
Any Branch

Each
Is a necessity
A niche narrowly nudging each other
Foreign peninsulas and inlets
Without hierarchy
Irreplaceably invested
In the machine
That makes
Uniforms Ungrateful

But not Ugly
shipping sailors
and marching soldiers
from raging poverty
to ragtag regimes

An Army
 of hopes and dreams
is better than being beaten
for being Black
Inhaling the
 Air
Forcing
Social mobility
To be the first in
The water with
Lifesaving Arrogance:
Devil Dogs swim too
But who guards
When the Coast isn't clear?

Self worth isn't shinier
From a sailing ship
A cockpit or
The hummer
Resilience still keeps dragging time
Taking months
Basic
Training
To unlearn
The illusion of obligation
Lapel pinned
And ranked
In Security

Homeland is more than
Stolen soil
When your obligation
Signed the contracts
In a dignity
Sworn
To find respect
In rank and reason

The Last Official Face

Jacque Jacobs

Blue eyes, shining with possibility and
perhaps a hint of flirtation beneath
your close-cropped blond hair
covered by your sailor's cap,
looked at the piece of paper assigning your duty station.

It was my job to be the last official face you saw at home
before you boarded that ship bound for Vietnam.

Those were my initials—carefully placed letters—
to the right of the Captain's rubber-stamped signature.

Both of us were young, perhaps both believers
in the country we served—whether by choice or conscription.

I imagined the wonder of the voyage ahead of you—
the wide undulating seas you would ride
so far from the cornfields that raised you.

More than fifty years have passed since my last official act.

Today your blue eyes and blond hair haunt my thoughts—
as I wonder if I sent you to defend a fragile liberty
or sent you to your death.

What Did You Do In The War, Daddy?

Rollin Jewett

What did you do in the war, daddy?
I dropped some bombs from way over head
On somebody else's shore
I shot at the enemy until they were dead
That's what I did in the war, sonny
That's what I did in the war

What did you see in the war, daddy?
I saw young soldiers losing their lives
And not really knowing what for
They orphaned their children and widowed their wives
That's what I saw in the war, sonny
That's what I saw in the war

Who did you kill in the war, daddy?
I killed some people that I never met
Just so we could even the score
But some of their faces I'll never forget
That's who I killed in the war, sonny
That's who I killed in the war

Why did you fight in the war, daddy?
I fought 'cus the government told me to fight
For reasons they kept obscure
They told us that what we were doing was right
That's why I fought in the war, sonny
That's why I fought in the war

How do you feel about war, daddy?
I wish I could tell you your daddy was proud
Of keeping his country secure
But all I can think of is all of the innocent
victims, and friends, and brothers, and husbands and fathers and sons....
That aren't with us any more
And that....yeah, that's what I did in the war.

A Colored Regiment Returns from WWI

Matthew Johnson

The colored regiment returned after the kings and kaisers
Ceased their marching orders
After leveling so much of the continent,
And so many innocent lives and homes.

James Reese Europe, on making it back to the States,
Resumes refining his sound at postwar gigs,
And passes the baton to black and brown bandleaders
And mentees in speakeasies,
Who push the tradition
After the death of the lieutenant and ragtimer.

Langston goes to these clubs and writes down what he sees
Into poems, letting the world know
That black people do know of things beyond dance and music,
Like love.

Wives, mothers, and newspapers
Welcome the returning soldiers.

Alain Locke declares there is a new Negro in America.

DuBois urges these men,
Who fit the billing of a Talented Tenth,
To shepherd the Hundreds.

News arrives that a man was lynched yesterday,
And another brown boy is murdered in the South;
His ashes had to be gathered at night.

Years of fighting and dying
Have not ended for black veterans,
But has merely moved oceans and to the home front.

The Jumper

Paul Jones

I first saw him as a meteor. His foot flare
blazing as he fell from the helicopter.
They became odd ornaments in an evergreen,
a camo-chute and matching camo-Marine.
I don't know why he stayed stuck up there;
snakes can shinny down a tree and so can bears.
But he seemed happy just to hang around.
Nonetheless, I reached up to help him down.
He said he had been raised in coal country.
All the men in his family worked in mines.
While he was suspended in the pine tree,
he was owned by air although he lost his shine.
How fresh the night tasted, how his lungs filled
with stars, how he never wanted to exhale.

Testimony of J. Sidney Setzer (1841-1916)

Paul Jones

I was not the bravest of the brave though
I participated in every engagement
my regiment engaged in (until captured.)
The battles of Gettysburg, Wilderness,
and Spottsylvania Court House being
the most disastrous. I witnessed a number
of our men torn asunder, threads of flesh
thrown into low limbs of over-hanging trees.
Half or more of our survivors were captured,
including myself. The loss of life was appalling.
Our captors nearly drunk, howled; "no quarters."
Interference of their officers saved
us from massacre. We were rushed through
their six lines of battle over more dead than
I ever witnessed elsewhere. We were conveyed to
Point Lookout, Md.; later to Elmyra, N. Y.,
suffering untold destitution at both places.
The hardships, dangers, etc., of the four years
were almost intolerable.
I am now in my 70th year, am in
comfortable circumstances. Wife still living.
five living children; all married and in fairly
good circumstances. Two children dead.
I am still in the mercantile business.

At What Cost

Melissa Kelley

I conformed
I made myself act think work like you

I hid my feminine side

But it didn't disappear
For that side is the source of my strength

Conformity let me in
Womanhood fueled my power

While the mantle of maledom rested across my shoulders
Wrapping me in its brash banter, posturing and workaholic go go go
I walked a tightrope, barely balanced

But there was a cost
A constant questioning of which part of me deserved to be seen
A constant questioning of which part of me was really me

I am still paying that bill

The Bombs Bursting in Air

Anne Kissel

Searing soulless August heat settled
like a shroud on the dressed up crowd
filling the bleachers in the parade ground.
VIPs stacked in choice middle rows,
fifty yard line status for the brass and sass.
All stood, all pledged, all sat and waited.

The General, sandpaper voice,
face like a map, bellowed his welcome
to officers, troops, dependents and
somehow important civilians.
This was the Home of Armor, he said,
but today was about air and sky.
(tanks did not well suit this far away war)

Helicopters buzzed by; giant gnats
stirring dust, ruffling dresses, gunners
hanging like spiders from open sides.
Bullets and bullets and bullets
poured on the dry green field,
(Pock! Pock! Pock!)
left little volcanoes of dirt and turf.

Show-off F-4s streaked low and sleek.
Trailing blades of shadeless clouds,
their fierce screams pushed hands to ears.

Like a July Fourth finale, reliable chugging
B-52s dropped samples of Napalm.
The ground seared with heat and awe,
cooling the day in contrast.

Ears ringing, acrid smoke slyly clinging,
bodies tingling, minds puzzled, hearts full,
guests greeted their soldiers below.
What did they just see?
A play? A game?
An affirmation of might? Or right?
Who won?

What Feeds the Wheat

Carol Krauss

Wheat tresses unfurl for near a mile.
Hard to imagine a battle was fought
on this field of amber. Nestled between
farmer fence and farmer fence.
Gettysburg 1863. Pickett's Charge.
The blood, bone of fallen soldiers,
nourish the soil, year after year.
And we bow our heads before breaking
bread. *This is my body that is for you.*
Do this in remembrance of me.

Lullaby

Rachel Landsee

We were at war, not in metaphor.
Skilled at manipulating the army, you arrived on a tasker,
Visiting my base just enough to earn us a honeymoon suite:
One-third of a containerized housing unit.

When you unpacked Christmas gifts,
Lingerie beneath bullets,
I remembered confusion in kindergarten:
Navigating children with new expressions,
Under too-bright fluorescent lights,
Lost without the security of home until my sister dropped in,
To return the other half of my heart.

She was at the same school.
You were in the same army.
You both made the air different.

We laid there, two single beds pushed together,
Laughing about the house we owned in peacetime,
Where we did not walk one minute and 24 seconds to a
communal bathroom,
Through a maze of T-walls. Where we did not awaken to the
C-RAM.
You slept in the crack.
Which existence was that?
You once said the only thing missing from Kurdistan was me.

Sometimes I dropped you off at a nondescript compound like everyday commuters.
I welcomed you back when you traveled around the country.
We curled close when we heard controlled detonations or other explosions,
Never knowing which was which.

In the New Year, you brought treats from the Green Zone.
Lemon soda from Germany,
Soft cheese from France,
La Vache Qui Rit, we bungled the last word.

Upon your departure, my unsafe heart emerged.
I stayed several more months, alone in a combat zone.
What should life look like now?

Less than a year later, after your yet another deployment,
We gave birth to her.

HOLD

Rachel Landsee

One thing war grants is close calls with life.
Interpretation is in the aftermath.

We served in two combat zones, six times in six years.
We overlapped, we divided, we interwove. Then we had a child.

I checked on her every time she rolled over in the night,
Every sigh, every breath.

You tried calming me with rationale,
But this was beyond reason.

You think you'd actually hear her last breath?
Yes.
And do what?
Run in.
And then what? You couldn't bring her back to life.
I'd find a way.
She's fine, get some sleep.

I stayed awake.

Years later I figured it out:
My first-year vigil was a manifestation of our close calls.
Because danger is both overt and concealed,
Because life is too precarious to comprehend.

Yet.

Even with the promise that runs with realization,
The beautiful aha of clarity in a moment,
Ten years and a lifetime later,
I still check on her through the night.

Possum Byers

Brenda Ledford

Harold was slow to anger.
A veteran of Vietnam,
he entered law enforcement.

Confident, an excellent marksman,
he taught Possum Byers
how to handle weapons

during the basic law class.
The strict instructor screamed
and pressured the students.

Possum asked Harold,
"Why doesn't he scream at you?"
The tall man chuckled

and with his deep voice
told the young man,
"Just yell back at him!"

Casualty Poem

Marc Levy

At dusk, what hand dropped the metal bulb
Down the narrow tube, lifting it skyward?
I was dreaming the moment the plummeting
Brightness struck, a dim noise, I was lifted
Floating above myself, below
The soft fiery puffs of mortar shells
The firefly tracer paths
The glow of skittering shrapnel
Then all at once
When I crashed down
This lifting gift upended.
In my absence, only my beating
Heart, everything breathing.
Turning about, I woke to help them
But stumbled, fell
The back of my head, my chest, too wet
Too warm for comfort. Someone
Held my arms, legs, pressed white cloth
Dim voices, "...not gonna make it."
Then waiting in the green trembling thing
Doctors and more blood, this time good.
A year of red dust, red rain.
Years to unlearn it.
Of late, in the hills where I live,
When the moon is low
The frozen sky flecked by starlight
In those still moments, by that hand
My darkness disarmed, I am uplifted.

Eighteen Years After He Died

Marc Levy

At first light Mike walks point across the flat dry field.
Behind him, the medic I once was, twenty-two barrel
Pointed south, our foot steps launching small white clouds.

We're hunting ground hogs, you understand,
Not like the green time, hunting each other down.
But today, under a bright Michigan sun
There'll be no shouts or body count.

In the distance, reactor stacks jut against the open sky.
In the eye of my mind I frame the scene, step into it,
Proclaim: Medic with rifle and nuclear power–
It's the perfect holiday card!

You wouldn't, says Mike.
I toss him my camera. Hold the pose.
Tell him, take the picture. Take it.

Click

That year my vet friends got the gag.
Most civilians didn't.
Patrol, jungle, ambush, monsoon—
What do they know of such things?

It grows late. Here's to Charles 'Mike' Wilson—
Third platoon RTO, loving father and husband,
Hard worker, avid sportsman, killer of ground hogs.
Lover of life.

Fort Bragg

Robert Lunday

Tonight I'm out walking the firing range
where Army brats used to fuck behind the targets.
We all loved each other—
we all had the same stewed brain.
I've stared at the stars so long my head's a sphere.
It rubs through space and time, it sees:
Brenda Lee in a blue sequined dress.
The ring of fire Johnny Cash sang from the Wurlitzer
promiscuous of song,
brainless in its lights.
Neon banking the boulevards,
bulb-strung car lots, teeth
knocked down a man's throat.
Mother pregnant smoking a Salem, the red tip going ash,
breaking and snowing over the floor.
Fathers falling under canopies, wild dust
as they hit the ground, collapsing
rainbows of the chutes, heat wrinkling the air
so they walk back through waves,
the rainbows gathered in their arms.
Fireflies in orbit around my jar.
Mother's face a haze behind the screen,
calling the flickering shapes of our names.
War games, copters, mortars,
machine guns in the hands of boys.
The young planets flung out to slow and cool.
A battalion of frogs,

all of us drunk, strung out behind the targets,
somebody crying, somebody throwing up,
the sudden quiet and what passes for sleep,
car radio cutting through it, news of Apollo
tracking to the moon.
I'm turning gray;
what does that make you?
Old man, come back from the moon.
Nobody goes there anymore.
Carry your rainbow rumpled in your arms again.
Bury it here.

Recruit Poem

Gabriel Maravelas

If this poem was a recruit
could you try and break it
make it want to fight
could you turn it into a war poem

could you turn it into the kind of poem
that brings in the fast movers
to crush the insurgency of the competing verses
a desperate twisting of words in search of victory

What about after
When you don't need so many war poems anymore
Could you print it out and stamp it
Leave it out on the derelict streets with an 800 number
written on it in pen with a sticky note
says "VA intake line"

Could you tell it that it needs to be a love poem now
That it needs to reintegrate itself into another kind of poem
That no one will accept for it to stay the same
That if it doesn't take well to these *edits* then
there are *medications* that can help

What about the poems that didn't make it back to the publisher?
Never got the chance to not be a war poem
Pencil scrawled lost forever in some small dusty notebook

Fallen out the open pocket of the poet's backpack, in some overseas land
Could you leave a blank page in the chapbook open for them?
Like a memory
For the war poems that will always be war poems

Rock My Boat

Gabriel Maravelas

The sky was there, it was just there
but blankish, features hard to distinguish
like the faces of the six grandfathers
before the settlers made Mt. Rushmore over it

under all this the boat was engulfed in its own empty dreams of potential
because there was no wind to send it anywhere
so it sat upon the flat water, canvas up, needlessly
demanding a luff in the sail, at least I was, a potential dictator

Then there was the wake from the passing motorboat
To induce a sort of rocking action into this cathartic scene
And, with a single loose halyard chiming in protest, the boat did
move a little bit, and like an old and tired dog it did rise
To bark around awhile before returning to a lump

But yet I was satisfied
To lay back with a foot on the tiller
And to think about the war
And to pointlessly trim the drooping jib
And to watch the stillness in the air
And to watch the wind indicator for a confirmation
That I wasn't going anywhere

The Thing

Marchiano

Chris isn't
really Chris
anymore.

Probably not
[myself anymore
either.

Stopped looking
in the mirror
except for when

you have
to. To
shave. To

acknowledge
that you
still pass off

as human.]
This Chris
isn't Chris.

That one
had a wife.
Two kids.

This one
has trouble forming
sentences.

This one
spent two
hours scrubbing
blood out of concrete.

A Hum in the Living Room

Lenard D. Moore

One morning Daddy, just home from Vietnam,
came in the living room and sat in his chair.
I sat waiting on the shabby stool,
hair clippers in my hand.
I turned the clippers on
before handing it to him.
It hummed like honeybees.
He jerked back against the chair.
It was the first time
he'd heard it hum in a year.
How terrible to see his face turn red,
and hear him gasping.
He gradually straightened up,
asked me to hold my head still,
and considered the part he wanted to cut.
I turned around on the stool,
frightened, squinting,
dreading the next haircut.

Grandmother on the Porch

Lenard D. Moore

A month after Father left us in khakis,
she came to visit us.
Words were fewer than usual.
All day she sat on the porch
facing the thick field of wavering corn.
When Mother went into the house to cook,
she turned toward me.
She whispered, "I keep thinking
of your Daddy in Vietnam."
I pushed my nine-year-old hands into my pockets
and said, "Me, too. I want him
to take me fishing again."
She dabbed her eyes and said,
"My son must have us on his mind."
Mother came to the door and stood,
with flour on her hands.
"If Daddy can't be here," I said,
Why can't I be him?"
Grandmother's eyes were a blank.

My Father Leaves for Vietnam

Lenard D. Moore

When my father let loose my mother
from his outstretched arms,
he stared into her eyes,
as if wanting to see his pain.
I had never seen him cry.
His eyes dammed the water.
I felt my mother's heart drumming in me.
He looked down and
whispered in my ear, "I'll be back,
don't be afraid,"
then he turned away.
He boarded the Greyhound.
I held my mother's hand and looked
at him climbing the steps.
He sat and hung his hand out the window.
I watched the bus fade.
I have never understood why he had to go,
although my mother cupped me in her arms,
as if she still could reach my father.

What Was Said on the Porch

Lenard D. Moore

When I was nine
my father stood
on the wooden steps of our porch
while the leaves of the maple
at the roadside
fell in whispers.
He thoughtfully asked my great uncle
to take care of Chicken.
Father had always called Mother "Chicken."
"Of course," Great Uncle said,
"I'll look out for my niece"
and glanced down at me.
I wanted to answer I'll take care
of Mother, but I knew my place.
"I don't know what Vietnam will be like,"
father told him, "I just don't know."
Great uncle turned his gaze
to the wind chimes that hung from the roof,
hat tilted the way of the wind,
and cigar burning red.
Father's eyes were red from crying,
his hands tucked in his pockets
as a change of air moved
between Great uncle and him.

Vietnam Haiku

Lenard D. Moore

after the ambush,
the dust settling
into the silence

a village woman
running across white-hot sand
her baby in hand

rifle rounds ended—
a flying squirrel leaps
from the jungle vines

the heat in the trench
a marine lifts the helmet
off his head

The Boys of Winter

Andrew Newby

I.
In the Second Battle of Fallujah, November 2004

we placed bets on how much you'd hate all of this,
all of you laying there. What could be brought home
on tax dollars and some plane

while half your widow waits, folded twice
on some chair like wet laundry, the other half
vanished some place she couldn't spell

before the rest of the family showed up
and asked *what city in Iraq is the war* and
are we still over there and *can you believe it.*

II.
there's something I learned from an Iraqi prisoner:
we both want the same thing
for us to go home
        and if not home, away
                        and if not away, everywhere.

III.
Before the others showed up we said things
like *you didn't feel as pink as you went out*
like the pink mist you became on account of them

but we aired them out
      for you
put holes almost all the way through them
wasted them because

IV.
after it's finished
there's a pile of boys,
and sometimes when they go
they go everywhere,

there are piles of someone's boy
across the way
who found what quiet there is
beneath the sprig of acacia

The Struggle is Real

Keith Ockimey

During my lifetime, I had the chance to experience a wonderful group of Care Providers, Veterans, and Artists. This group was formed for the betterment of me and my healing. Just like any other undertaking, the team rolled in slowly at first, and then gained momentum as our passions progressed. The only way to accomplish this was to establish an arena of peace (with LOVE being the central element). We then removed all judgment, prepared ourselves, and got to work! My memories were heightened every single day of the experience.

Allow me to share some of my observations and insights…

I remember when guilt had me frozen with fear,
Now peace and love guide my path.

I remember when intrusive thoughts invaded my head,
Now I WRITE to sing and change my mood.

I remember when encouraging others seemed like a menial task,
Now the fruits of my labor are a reason to celebrate.

I remember when bad dreams would not allow peaceful slumber,
Now occasionally, I sleep through the night.

I remember the emptiness of losing a loved one,
Now I use my memories as fuel to build new relationships.

I remember the kindness of my friends and strangers alike,
Now I return the kindness as often as I can.

I remember my youth and the strength that I possessed,
Now I exercise to reclaim my strength.

I remember making bad choices in the past,
Now I stop to consider making better choices.

I remember feeling lonely all the time,
Now I use my alone time to reflect upon my goals.

I remember not wanting to do anything at all,
Now I have enrolled in courses to challenge myself.

I remember failing at everything,
Now I succeed at things and don't worry about the rest.

I remember constant bad moods,
Now I have good days and GREAT days!

I remember always worrying about what others think of me,
Now whatever they think of me is none of my concern.

I remember not having any friends,
Now I talk to a buddy on the phone every night.

    I firmly believe that a community that cares for each other can strive and succeed…This is our destiny…a community of providers, Veterans, and artists…Let's call upon everyone to join us in order to expand and fulfill our legacies!

I Feel Happy

Keith Ockimey

I experience elation at the time of awakening.
I have joy when I think about what He's done for me.
I become gleeful at the Art Museum.
I get excited chills from women artists.
I get uplifting vibes from life in general.
I become pleasure filled at the time of completion.
I get contentment from positive experiences.
I'm delighted by the joys of summer.
I get enjoyment from loving experiences.
I get good spirits from Veterans that unite.

#MouthOfaMarine #MarineCorpsMade #PTSD #PenNamedMe #CPMaze

Charles Perry Jr. "C.P. Maze"

2 tours
2 Sea Service Deployment Ribbons
Armed Forces Expeditionary Medal
Nato Medal
Good Conduct Medal
Armed Forces Service Medal
Certificate of Commendation
Meritorious Commendation
Rifle Expert Shooting Badge
3 of my Band of Brothers never made it home alive
another a failed Suicide attempt
2 murder trials

#MouthOfaMarine #MarineCorpsMade
#PTSD #PenNamedMe #cpmaze

Have you ever made a Goddess bite her lip
Made splinters jump off the cross through His wrist
Made from a Carpenter's son's last suppers' tooth pics
I am the razor blade that razor blades shave with

#MouthOfaMarine #MarineCorpsMade

I'm a thunderstorm I'm a tornado
I'm a Category High 5 God
I'm a Marine I'm a *muthafucking* Hurricane
I'm an *"I don't give a good goddamn"*
trapped in an *"I don't give a fuck's"* body

tell the mirror
to tell *Darkness*
that last year
I just couldn't afford
God's light bill

stop fist fighting *Lightning* over lightning (((*maze*)))
stop misplacing your prescription shot glasses (((*maze*)))
stop doing doughnuts tipsy drunk around her halo
(((maze)))
& stop playing with your penis
as if it's a pinata a pretty girl
can knock the candy right out of

make no mistake
her matchstick mouth's *Beautiful*
as if it was a second chance
in a second language to
speak liquid sexy skin fluently

Hey Hashtag

I hung my halo
on the coat rack
in her smile & begged
vocal chords in her heart's
string session skin
to sweat me a symphony

oh believe me Beautiful
I left cave paintings
inside the walls of women
& walked away from them
with whiskey on my breath
& water turned into wine
in my liver

fresh kept razors kept in medicine cabinets
kept open doors above your wrist
kept ashtrays filled with charred cigarette butts
filled with cute stoner half lipstick-stained joints
empty high-end beer bottles on the kitchen counter
& four stained Malbec & Merlot wine glasses
laying fetal positions in the kitchen sink

all of our former lives
held their lighter fluid hands together
as they burned bridges & flags
in our name

I Will Wear Sandals with Socks

David W. Plunkett

I will wear sandals with socks,
walk about in a straw hat,
steadying myself upon a cane,
and, retiring from my journey to this dock,
sit and await the ending of today.
I will dangle my feet above the water
and shade my eyes with freckled hands
as I observe the joint of two worlds.
Green mountains and cloud-marbled sky
will rise and lie (which is real?)
until a passing boat breaks the lake,
roiling the false heaven with its wake,
the riders waving as they go by,
free for a moment from their workplace
and mindless of how they interrupt my reflection.
I will watch the gyre of the agile swallow.
The stately heron will stalk the far shore
patiently fishing for small fry.
I, too, will look for fish in the shallows
but see only my aging face stretch and waver
in the chop of broken glass.
Was I ever other so?
Another afternoon arises.
I am with my friends.
The bay shimmers silver and grey
split by the last shafts of a retiring sun.

As we bob atop a wooden raft,
that is tied against the ship we have been painting,
young sailors, having set work aside,
our open shirts showing hairless chests of lately boys,
we push back white dixie cup hats,
doff scuffed boondockers and socks,
roll pants legs, and sinking bare feet into the cool water,
bait hooks with stale bread
then turn to the patient task of fishing.
Across the bay, the city waits.
We talk and laugh and pay
scant attention to the buildings rising
between us and the sinking day.
We will walk those streets soon enough.
But for now, we hold up our catch
and tout our prowess as fishermen
as if that is all we will ever need do,
all I ever dream of doing.

Memorial Day, My Son Leaves Home

Barbara Presnell

Not long after he has pulled out of the driveway and gone,
I walk by myself to the courthouse square
where a small group has gathered, some circling
the monument to the Confederate dead,
others seated in plastic folding chairs
opened in formation along the Main Street curb.
A light mist has begun to fall. At the microphone
a man in a red VFW jacket reads from an unfolded paper,
his mouth so close to metal his words muffle.
I stand back from the group
because I am not a veteran or the wife of a veteran
just a daughter of one long gone and the mother
of a boy I pray will never see a battlefield.
To my right is a man whose gray hair collapses
at his shoulders. His ragged beard, his tarnished skin
and milky eyes scream *Vietnam, Vietnam.*
As each wreath of war is lowered to the ground,
I imagine that my son must have passed
through Raleigh by now, must be driving east
beside new tobacco fields and corn
just beginning to green up from the earth.
Seven muskets fire three times, their smoke
blending into fog. Then "Taps." Beside me,
standing at attention and saluting the damp air,
the gray vet cries. As the bugle's echoes fade,
I imagine my son's arm, strong and brown,
resting in an open window,
his shirt sleeve flapping in the wind.

WHAT FLUTTERS

Barbara Presnell

      Heat rising. Tick of afternoon sun.
The screen door, banging. A telegram.
When it comes, Hannah is in the kitchen making dinner.
She slips her greased finger beneath the flap,
hands trembling so she can hardly read.
      Company almost wiped out. Stop. Our boys
      fought bravely to the end. Stop.
It's the *almost* she clings to as day splinters
into days, then a week.

      Wings tipping. Grass that pillows.
Loose fabric. A place called France—she's seen it on a map
and Slim sent a postcard back in July.
Words. Picture of a cow in a field like theirs.
Bone jur scribbled above the cow's ear.
Seems like a fine place on the back side. And,
      Everybody says hi. I sure miss
      your cold ice tea, Mama.

      Flotilla of red leaves. Fine hairs
of a sweet potato. Screen door
banging. Her husband Josiah holds the letter.
He's alive. Our boy. Then names those gone:
      the Dixon's youngest, Jimmy Gatlin,
      Big John Pugh. More.
His gray chin on her shoulder.
Dusk stirring in.

Planting the Garden

Barbara Presnell

Last fall, four boys stood
on the back porch like snipers,
steadied b.b. guns on the rail,
and fired at G.I. Joes propped on fence posts.
Now body parts of dead soldiers
lie fallow in dirt like volunteer radishes
and I don't know what I am raising.

These are boys whose skin is smooth as young squash.
War is only what they read about
under covers when the house is still,
dying young is plastic soldiers
gasping in the bean rows.

I pause, my hoe a makeshift crutch,
and cradle a toy face in my hand.
I touch the brown eyes,
the perfect part of hair,
straight as fence wire, just right of the middle.
So like my son's.

I lay him down,
tuck him in soil.

Why Pronouns Matter

Pat Riviere-Seel

We've all done stupid things
but most don't follow us around
like stray dogs, tail wagging,
tongue lolling, eyes pleading,
pet me. Pet me. Pet me. Pay
attention, like the time he
slammed the car door on his
sister's fingers. A thoughtless
accident, adolescent carelessness.
Fingers bruised, but intact,
she forgave him. Not so
that day on patrol when he
tossed a grenade into a shelter,
watched the top lift, wondered,
too late, *what* he had shattered
into dust. Fifty years later
he still can't say, *who*...

FIREPOWER

Pat Riviere-Seel

On the best nights she wakes slowly,
floating up from dreams, his hand
brushing hair from her face,
his eyes imploring her to open hers,
the whole house blazing with light.

Ice cream? He offers, perched
beside her, bowl cradled in his hands.
Other nights his screams wake her. Once
she found a pistol stashed
behind the sofa cushions. *Not loaded,*
he shrugged when she complained.

Each day a little more of his grin
disappears, the field of freckles across his nose fades,
the dimple on his left cheek absorbed now
into a permanent scowl. It's been months
since he laughed. The summer before he left
they bought fireworks, lit them on the beach,
blasting the quiet, arousing sleeping dogs
as brilliant flashes lit a moonless sky.
Afterward, they slept, spooned in salt and sand.
Now he winces at her touch. When she discovers
the gun in the nightstand, he takes it from her,
his face unreadable as he gathers the words,
I'm going back.

How Could I Not

Gina Singleton

How could I not?
How could I ignore the obvious?
You spoke your words and pain hit me
It wasn't my pain, it was yours
Your words were a cry to anyone who could hear
Did you really think it wasn't obvious?
We are different in many ways
Your male to my female
Your white to my brown
Your south to my north
Your Navy to my Marine Corps
Despite all that we are bound by honor
We both raised our right hands
We both gave years to defend our country
We both returned with invisible scars
Does your family hear your pain?
Mine can't be bothered
Does your family understand your sacrifice?
Mine only thinks of the years I gave
Does your family realize that you are alone?
Mine tries to convince me I'm crazy
We don't share blood, we share honor
We don't share blood, we share sacrifice
We don't share blood, we share understanding
You are my brother by bond
My brother I hear your pain

My brother I'll be here to lean on
My brother cry your tears and I'll call it rain
My brother regardless of the distance you'll never be alone

Dear Military Child

Gina Singleton

You are brave, sweet and loved. Yes, my job took me away from you for a few months but I will call often and be back as soon as they let me. Never forget that you are strong and braver than other kids your age. The other kids do not have to get up before the sun to get to daycare or get home so late at night that mommy is cooking dinner with her work clothes on. Those other kids will never know how much it hurts to see mommy/daddy leave and leave you behind for a few months. Do you think that those kids know the pain of getting a call but still having to wait a long time to hug mommy/daddy again? None of those kids have to worry about the war that is going on so far away from home. As you grow you do this a few more times. You are no longer the sweet innocent happy child from before, now you are angry. You're angry that mommy/daddy had to go away again and will miss another birthday. You are angry that you have to leave your friends behind and start school in a different state. Inside you ache from not feeling normal, like all the other kids that don't have a military parent. On one hand you wish you were them but you are also proud about what your parent does. Through your anger, hurt, silence and tears know that I do not leave you because I no longer love you, I leave you because I must. Never forget that you are my heart living outside of my body and I need you to stay safe. I need you to continue to be well behaved and responsible as you always are. Help grandma out around the house and allow yourself to enjoy life. Nowhere in this world are kids braver than the military kids here. You are strong, resilient and loving. Here I must end this letter and if there is one thing that I need you to do while I'm gone it's to be a kid. Smile, laugh, play and enjoy every day. You are never far from my thoughts and always in my heart.

Mom/Dad

Drip

Cindy B. Stevens

I float above disquiet
mechanics, mothers, architects, fathers, farmers, children
dead

sun drenched flowers bemoan blood spilled fields
war swallows life
purpose

I dream dew trampled grass
I mourn homes
forests
farms
war drinks death

my moon sky is still
I breathe
wake
my battle mates don't, they're
stagnant

a hawk shadow dances a slow waltz
grey clouds promise rain
drown light
field hospital speakers dribble music
I can't massage my left knee ache

somebody
gather tap water from the faucet drip
the hand-washing sink
sprinkle my face
lips
drag fingers through my matted hair
I want my wife

I need to snuggle my children
in our rocking chair
read bedtime stories
blow belly raspberries
soak up their giggles

scratchy sheets tangle my feet
can I uncover?
will I deplore what I see
what I can't
see

No Return War

Cindy B. Stevens

when I didn't come back from war, my family grieved
they held onto hope
that my missing wasn't a departure
that my missing was only regret to inform
whereabouts unknown

my superiors passed platitudes
I was brave
I was courage
I was hero
but there was no POW medal for me
no dog tags
there was no body

my family went through my belongings
my photos
my clothing
my mementos: foreign stamps, coins
we don't always know the people closest to us

they sorted
distributed
cataloged
packed, labeled, and stored boxes in the spare bedroom closet
donated the rest of my stuff to the Rescue Mission

my chaplain tried to help
but it's something a family has to do
they all wondered about the small wooden box
metal hinges
a simple lock
silk lined

inside it smelled
like
sweaty pennies
it was empty
except for a photo
of a small child from a worn-torn country
with my wavy hair

Battlefield

Lee Stockdale

Balm of silence,
the cannons have stopped,
chaff of DD 214s
float into my foxhole,
with the smell of rifle bore cleaner,
and the vision of a woman
handing me five yellow daisies.

This silence, how long?
One minute. Twelve hours.
Is it still a battlefield?
Has history ended?

I see fellow soldiers,
disinterested and tired,
rise and walk toward the horizon,
silhouetted against distant fires.

I should join them,
but I have my orders:
I will guard everything
within the limits of my post,
and not quit my post
until properly relieved.

Low gray clouds
slide above me like coffins.
A stranger approaches,
peers into my foxhole,
hands down a message:
Your war is over.

Black Stones

Gina Streaty

He brought back Vietnam.
Verdant, sticky
fatigues on the back of a chair,
worn black boots
hunched like shiny cats
in a corner

Before he lifted his rag
stained with inky polish,
he touched it, in piercing rain,
in brothers dropping blood,
in just-rolled joints

Floating in upturned helmets
filled with muddy water,
he found tatty pages of letters
to someone's King

He touched Vietnam
where contorted mouths
gulped warm beer,
screamed with James Brown
While bullets tore their skin,
their women climbed darkness,
drifted back to faraway homes

He touched Vietnam.
With a handful of black stones
gathered from tangled rice grass,
his mother lines the mantle
where his picture leans at parade rest

What clings to soles
the black rag misses

A Letter Home

Gina Streaty

Dank Thursday morning
dingy hue of day-old dishwater
Postman totes a thin white lie,
stamped, postmarked
bordered in red, white, and
Air Force blue

APO San Francisco 96358
in loathsome cursive curls
Like a psychic's omen
this too will be dismissed, scratched
away like yesterday's crusted yolk
coating pink cabbage roses on
porcelain plates

Chipped, brittle nails and
calloused hands shred white bread
as stale and plenteous as last week's prayers,
moisten and knead, then prop this patriotic thing
behind the brass topped sugar bowl—a wedding gift—
until facts blur like penned words viewed
through bubble glass

Grits and eggs, hot sausage, bread pudding, sun tea
made with daybreak rainwater caught in tarnished tin
pans, poured into patterned paper cups for no one special

fragile like this day \ this breach \
this *thing* kneading *and needing,*
tucked and sealed in paper, still, in battle
until what is presumed useless and close to rot
gets reconstructed by listless toil, and time
like a pile of stale bread
reborn in hellish heat

Song: A Balm for the Decades

Gina Streaty

Haints hover over a lake of fire
haunt a weary infantry
as a Buddhist monk burns
at a Market in Saigon, sun-like, sacred
Any Day Now
bullets ricochet, grenades trounce
trenches, bunkers belch out bodies
near paddy fields stocked
with riddled remains
'60's shed those tears *Can I Get a Witness?*
      '72: Peace out brotha!
      These eyes hunt brick houses, stone
      foxes, and foxy mamas—not Charlie
      Lust for sugar lips, cocoa
      hands, and nimble hips to
      Pop That Thang! (You Ought to Be With Me!)
      As bell bottoms fan dance floor flames
      bulbous butts and bosoms lie
Soldier boy oh my little soldier boy I'll be true to you
Letter Full of Tears, ink-scratched on frayed pages
tucked in bloody threadbare fatigues,
jungle weeds, and delivered stateside with dog tags
Strange I Know
Hard Way to Go
    Now backs hunch, lean low
    Pelvises heave   Slide, baby, roll
    'cause Freddie's Dead—

(and Ernest and Calvin, Robert, Eddie, David, Jr., Allen,
Marcus, Lewis, Vinny, Earl-Dean, Paul,
Leroy, Marshall, Jeffrey ...Walter, Kenneth, Joseph, Bo...)
I saw souls ascend from a palette of green
to incandescent arms and fly
    Slippin' Into Darkness
near two dead missionaries between Da Lat and Saigon
    Oh Girl, roll away the stone
    slide, baby, roll
Do Your Thing
    Peace my mind   Still my bones
    Napalm nightmares
    Squelch the screams
    Play *Lean On Me* (or *I'll Take You There!*)
I'm Just Another Soldier
    Please, make me the theme from *Trouble Man*

Desert Storm

Gina Streaty

Longed for parcel from a pen pal
      in Virginia
Lucky Strikes in a battered boot
Upturned helmet gulps rare rain

In a Saudi desert

For a moment
on this couch cradled in its sag
      I wince
As sand and shrapnel pelt me
a shamal scrapes the floodplain
of the Tigris and Euphrates,
seeks New England leaves swirling
in amber death throes
Outside this temporary prison
of double-pane windows
a backdrop of stratus-strewn blue
I am nine on Grandpa's knee
seven in pigtails in a bathtub with Barbie
three reciting John 11:35 in Sunday school
zero, hope intact in a teenage womb

    for a moment

The peck-peck-tap of a restless pen against a notebook
Green marbles oscillate behind tortoiseshell frames
prod my back, fish for formulaic phrases
then hook my hard palate
as I rub a phantom pain
empty myself and de-crease
half the couch

Nothing left
to do except sit \
eyes drawn \ head bowed
in my room \ on my Air Hawk chariot
until next week's session
until my dry mouth births another wail
amid the searing soupy stench
of war, stale coffee, and office odors,

killing time

The Skin of Things

Edward Supranowicz

Once it was smooth,
Then it was torn.

Blood that was hidden
Flowed on the outside.

And what is left is
A jagged line, a scar.

But healing is and was
Never quite perfect –

The past cannot be undone,
But life can be stitched together.

The War

Ric Vandett

From a noble beginning
To an ignoble end
It parted the nation
As Moses parted a sea

Overnight boys became men
And men died
Politicians argued in Congress
And men died
Students protested in college
And men died
Jane visited Hanoi
And men died
Nixon replaced Johnson
And men died
The sixties became the seventies
And men died

Gone was the reason to go there
Gone was the resolve to stay there

Winning was not as important
As surviving a year

And we went home
To a nation divided

New Man

Daniel Walter

My pain lived within
I gave all I could give
My body it barely moved
And nothing I tried would sooth

Anger was the only thing I felt
I thought a wrong hand I was dealt
That nothing I would do would change
No way life could be rearranged

But God had found meaning in my soul
And warmed me up when I was cold
He found worth in my scars
And reminded me He made the stars

Trauma changed the way I see
But everything that happened made me, me
Peace was found when I forgave myself
Live in now and no where else

So now I tell you I am strong
I am forgiven for all my wrong
My life is great from where I stand
Today you see a brand new man

How the Shadow Hits Me

Daniel Walter

As I sit beneath this tree
I wonder how the shadow hits me
How the wind moves away
Yet here I stay

My thoughts of a past denied
And thoughts of a future hard to find
It is the tree that takes my mind
And how the shadow hits me

For rivers run into the sea
Mountains climb above me
Valleys look away
And here I stay

My eyes look not to the sky
Or down below the earth tonight
They gaze upon the mighty tree
And how the shadow hits me

My lungs they fill with air
My heart beats letting me know it's there
Moments pass and still, I stare
At how the shadow hits me

The birds they do not fly
The darkest clouds fill the sky
Each step is a question why
And how the shadow hits me

Gazing at the stars you imagine how little we are
That so much above and far below yet here we stand that's all we know
I imagine galaxies far away and what creatures on them play
Waters flowing and air to breathe in the places not yet seen
How small we are to all there is but in this thought peace now lives
For we have power over ourselves how we think and where we dwell

We think of happiness as thought, not action, but it is how we reach happiness that we must remind ourselves of. Those actions pave the road to forgiveness. Actions that are in defiance of our very thought. Actions that bring us to a place of surrender take what we have given as a gift, not a curse. We follow this road to a destination that reminds us that we are human. Reach for those thoughts that bring you closer to the destination you deserve. Fight back against your mind when it shows you what you can't do by doing that very thing. Mistakes are made but they do not make us. Grab ahold of that happiness you reach for. Do not let it slip through your fingers as your mind wanders and looks for something else to believe in.

Packed Away

Michael White

The unseen, unheard, & unknown.
18&53
I push the magazine release & the all so familiar sound of metal
sliding on metal as it falls in my left
hand,
And with my right I position the first one in between my thumb
and pointer
An unknown round of broken relationships just the first of
many, they didn't ask, nor did I know what to
tell them out of ignorance,
A second round this one is hot much like my temper,
The 3rd, a round of self-medication that would last what seemed
like a lifetime,
The next, was clean, just like the many stays impatient,
This round was a bit hard to see, much like myself, years the one
that cared never knew where I was,
This round was expensive, much like all the lawless deeds that
was paid for,
This round was wet, just like all the tears shed,
There's a round missing, much like a void in my life,
This round is red I suppose for the 53 dead that didn't get to
come home
One by one I pack them in the magazine
The next one getting tighter
For the next ten years I would shoot and reload these rounds
Oh God the people I've hurt

Till finally one day there's no more, rounds, or people in my sights
There's a power greater than myself, if it had a hand, it laid it on mine and I finally lowered this way to
hurt others and myself, oh God what have I done?

Only A Dream

Tanya Whitney

I sit alone, searching.
Gazing into a dark abyss.
Seeing images from long ago,
Fuzzy, yet clear.

Cars pass on the road,
But I can't hear them
Over the explosion of gunfire.
Deafness pervades.

Birds fly in the air,
Like tracer rounds whizz by.
Lighting up the black night.
Fire with no flame.

Hot, stifling summer nights.
Ashes fall like winter snow,
Raining down in a tempest.
Puddles of death.

Playful yells of children
Transform to screams of agony
As their bodies turn red
With blood, not paint.

The dawn begins to rise
Bringing light into the dark abyss,
Chasing away black memories, death.
Blink away the fear.

A soft tap on the shoulder.
A reminder you aren't alone.
A soft whisper amidst the mind's chaos.
It's only a dream.

What Can I Say

Tanya Whitney

What can I say
to make you see me,
for the person I was
is not the person I am now.

What can I say
to make you understand
my life is broken into tiny
pieces shattered on the ground.

What can I say
to make it evident that
the heart you once loved
no longer beats in this shell.

What can I say
to regain your trust
when you no longer know
the person standing before you.

What can I say
to make things right
when everything is so wrong
and I alone am to blame.

What can I say
to explain the horrors
I witnessed as a soldier
as a person ordered to kill.

My Father's Gift

Katherine Wolfe

In my hand I hold a black metal
lunchbox with a rounded top
for a thermos of hot coffee.
In front of me, linotype machines
floor to ceiling, spew hot metal words.

At one machine, my father sits,
fingers on the keyboard moving
like a maestro composing a symphony,
fingers that a few years before
held a gun in the last of the world wars.

He sits now at peace setting type
for tomorrow's newspaper, a trade
he learned as a boy from his father.
I, anxious to leave the heat and noise,
quickly hand the lunchbox to him.

But he stops, wants to talk,
reward me for my long walk
up steps to the composing room,
reward me with a line of type,
my full name in molten metal.

While the type cools, he talks
of his labor union and shows me
his card with pride. In my hand,
I hold the type set by his hands,
his gift that still remains with me.

Father's Hands

Bob Wood

My father's hands, wrinkled, crooked, scarred,
and bent from a life of toil, worry and want:

I often wondered if his hands could talk,
what stories they would tell.

But wondering takes precious time from life,
no time to dwell.

Days are passing. It's my time at last
to look at my hands and remember the past.

I wonder if my son, an old man to be,
when looking at his hands,
will be reminded of me.

CONTRIBUTORS

Maureen Alsop, PhD lived and worked in North Carolina in the mid-90s and is the daughter of a WWII veteran. Her poems in this anthology appeared as a video at *Plants Painting Poetry,* in her recent poetry collection *Arbor Vitae* (Nauset Press), and in her debut novel, *Today Yesterday After My Death* (Erratum Press). She is the author of seven poetry collections including: *Apparition Wren*; *Mantic; Later Knives & Trees*; *Tender To Empress*; *Mirror Inside Coffin*; and *Pyre*.

John Balaban is the author of fourteen books of poetry and prose, which have won The Academy of American Poets' Lamont Prize and a National Poetry Series Selection. His poetry has received two nominations for the National Book Award. His most recent book is *Passing through a Gate: Poems, Essays, and Translations* (Copper Canyon Press, 2024). His *Locusts at the Edge of Summer: New and Selected Poems* won the 1998 William Carlos Williams Award from the Poetry Society of America. Among his publications are poems in *The Atlantic, The New York Review of Books, The Hudson Review, Granta,* and *Little Star*. Balaban is Emeritus Professor of English at North Carolina State University in Raleigh. He spent two years of Selective Service in Vietnam during the war.

Sam Barbee has a new collection, *Uncommon Book of Prayer* (2021, Main Street Rag). His previous poetry collection, *That Rain We Needed* (2016, Press 53), was a nominee for the Roanoke-Chowan Award as one of North Carolina's best poetry collections of 2016. He received the 59th Poet Laureate Award from the North Carolina Poetry Society for his poem "The Blood Watch"; and is a two-time Pushcart nominee.

LeJuane (El'Ja) Bowens is an award-winning spoken word artist, poet, speaker, and author. El'Ja Bowens has done work with the John Kennedy Center of the Performing Arts along with featuring at many festivals including the National Folk Festival, Big Ears Festival, and Arts in the Heart of Augusta Festival. He is the founder/director for the Southeast Regional NC Poetry Festival in Fayetteville, NC, and he has featured on Poetry Slam Inc and All Def Poetry on YouTube. He is the author of the books, *So Many Things to Say, Anywhere But Here, Blerd Lines, 3:10: A Poetic Journey through Life Hacks, BLACKout,* and *Before: A Collection of Poems.* www.poetrynmotionnc.com

Shana Brushaber is a military veteran who served in the USAF from 2000 to 2009.

Arlin Buyert is a Navy veteran and a poet.

Kellie Cannon is a poet, writer, and teacher living in Easton, Massachusetts, though she lived and taught military members, veterans, and their families in North Carolina for almost decade while her husband served in the US Army. She received her BA from Franklin Pierce in NH and her MFA in Creative Writing from Emerson College in Boston. She currently teaches at Curry College in Massachusetts, where she lives with her three children, husband, and Airedale Terriers: Twyla and Rose. Her poetry has been previously published in *Wilderness House Literary Review, Ballard Street Poetry Review, Kennesaw Review,* and *Fresh Lit.*

Melanie Costa served in the Marine Corps for four year and the Army Reserve for six years, deploying to Iraq for in 2003. She was a gunner on a team of all men, attached to a unit that had only four other females. She now works at the Providence, VA Medical Center as a Certified Peer Support Specialist, helping other Veterans recover.

Doug Croft is a community development leader and not-for-profit fundraising director. He lives in Charlotte from where he works, writes, and travels to see as many of his favorite rock 'n' roll bands as possible.

Tom Davis' publishing credits include *Poets Forum, The Carolina Runner, Triathlon Today, Georgia Athlete, The Fayetteville Observer's Saturday Extra, A Loving Voice Vol. I and II, Special Warfare,* and Winston-Salem Writers' *POETRY IN PLAIN SIGHT* program for 2013 and 2021. He has authored several books. Tom, a retired Special Forces Soldier, has completed his memoir, *The Most Fun I ever Had With My Clothes: On A March from Private to Colonel.* He lives in Sylva, NC.

Deborah H. Doolittle has lived in lots of different places, but now calls Jacksonville, North Carolina, home. A Pushcart Prize nominee, she is the author of *FLORIBUNDA*, a poetry collection, and three chapbook collections, *NO CRAZY NOTIONS, THAT ECHO,* and *BOGBOUND.* Some of her poems have recently appeared (or will soon appear) in *CLOUDBANK, THE JOURNAL* (Wales)*, KAKALAK, TWO HAWKS, SLANT, THE STAND,* and in audio format on *THE WRITER'S ALMANAC.* She shares a home with her husband, a retired Marine, four rescued cats, and a backyard full of birds.

Tiffani Deneen Fields writes to return anything stolen, to inspire and empower. She writes for the underdog, outcast, overachiever, survivor and renewed believer. Tiffani believes in the power of words, scribed and spoken, to invoke action and advocacy for any healing, recovery journey. She stands by the power of respect, vulnerability, authenticity, and transparency to foster healing. Tiffani is a United States Army veteran hailing from Baltimore, Maryland. She enjoys singing, dogs and everything art.

The winner of the 2024 Faulkner-Wisdom Poetry Prize, **Janet Ford** has published work in *Witness: Appalachia to Hatteras 2024, North Carolina Literary Review Online, Poetry East,* and *Caesura* among other publications. In 2017 she received the Guy Owen Prize from *Southern Poetry Review*. She makes her home in western North Carolina.

Michael Garofolo served as an Army Aviator. While on active duty, he was introduced to therapeutic journaling in a recovery course and found it extremely valuable in his recovery. Much of his writing draws from leaving the military and his continued journey of life.

John Gosslee served in the Air Force from 2003-2006, and in a combat zone for 15 months. He worked in ammunitions, and received the Air Force Achievement Medal for meritorious service while stationed in combat. He has had poetry published in *Poetry Ireland Review, Southampton Review, Yale Review,* and many other magazines. His latest book of poetry is *Fish Boy* (Nomadic Press, 2018). His website is www.johngosslee.com

Siren Hand served as a Geospatial Imagery Intelligence Analyst & Drill Sergeant in the US Army for nine years, and now attends Indiana University/Purdue University Indianapolis for Creative Writing/Medical Sociology, working towards Poetic and Narrative Therapy. Siren co-runs Antiquated Arts Society, a creative literary arts project that incorporates typewriters and vintage touches into community events. Siren has been featured in *genesis arts & literary magazine, The After Action Review,* and *THAT Literary Magazine*.

Eva Helton is the wife of retired Army and NC National Guard Veteran, Levi Helton. He was active in Vietnam in 1968-1969 during the Tet Offensive. He also served during Desert Storm. He is 100% disabled with Diabetes and Parkinson's Disease with Dementia from Agent Orange.

She had the distinct privilege to take his place in a Vietnam Writers workshop for the Healing of PTSD supported by the Asheville VA and Appalachian State University. There, she was able to tell some of his stories and also express some of the pain they have gone through and are experiencing now as a result of his service to his country.

Mary Hennessey is a vet from Fort Sam Houston who worked chiefly on an orthopedic ward, and occasionally, on the amputee ward. Her years as an Army Nurse were in many ways beyond language. These poems are evidence that she continues to try to find the words.

Virginia Ewing Hudson, a long-time resident of Raleigh, NC, now resides in New Mexico. After a hand injury in 1995, she briefly paused her intense career as a performing cellist and began writing. She bought a remote campsite in Northern NM as a place to retreat, and there, she became friends with some folks who fought in Vietnam. Conversations around late night campfires lead to furious roadside scribbling on drives home. She is a Thomas Wolfe Fiction Prize winner with work published in their journal. Bosque Press nominated her fiction for the Pushcart Prize. Virginia has published poetry in *Wildflower Muse, Verse Virtual, Women Speak*, and *Vision and Voice*.

Elizabeth W. Jackson is a practicing psychologist and writer with poems published in anthologies and literary magazines including *Crab Orchard Review, Poet Lore, Spillway*, and *The Southern Poetry Anthology Volume VII: North Carolina*. Individual poems have won regional awards or been finalists in national contests, and in 2018, Plan B Press published her chapbook, *River of Monuments*.

Lavinia Jackson served 5.5 years in the USCG. When she was stationed both in Boston, MA and Elizabeth City, NC, she wrote poems on active duty. She continued to write after she was honorably discharged. Poetry has been more than therapeutic. For Lavinia, it's how she engages with community, especially with fellow Veterans. She is currently an MFA student at Lenoir Rhyne University.

Jacque Jacobs, a retired professor of educational leadership from Western Carolina University, served in the U.S. Navy in the mid-1960s at the Naval Air Station-Norfolk. She was distinguished in July 1966 as the first female "Sailor of the Month." She has recently published her debut novel, *High on a Mountain,* the first of six books in her series, *Love is a Cabin.* Her stories are rooted in the tradition of Smoky Mountain storytellers.

Rollin Jewett is an award winning playwright, screenwriter, singer/songwriter, poet and author. Mr. Jewett's poetry has recently been seen in *Gathering Storm, Coffin Bell, Penumbra, Southern Fried Autopsies, Night Picnic,* and *Door is a Jar* Magazine. His short stories have been published in magazines and anthologies, including *Aphotic Realm, Fell Beasts and Fair, Fantasia Fairy Tales,* and *Bloodlet.* Mr. Jewett's plays have been produced off-Broadway and all over the world. Mr. Jewett lives in NC, and his poems come from a song he wrote and his grandfather, father and brother, who were all in the US military.

Matthew Johnson is the author of the poetry collections, *Shadow Folks and Soul Songs* (Kelsay Books), *Far from New York State* (New York Quarterly Press), and the chapbook, *Too Short to Box with God* (Finishing Line Press). His work has appeared or is forthcoming in *The African American Review, Front Porch Review, London Magazine, Maudlin* House, and elsewhere. Recipient of Best of the Net and Pushcart Prize nominations, as well as recognitions from the Hudson Valley Writers Center, Sundress Publications, Grand View University, he is the managing editor of *The Portrait of New England* and poetry editor of *The Twin Bill.* matthewjohnsonpoetry.com

Paul Jones is for the most part dull and uninteresting, but through imagination and craft he has managed to write poems that have appeared in *Hudson Review, Tar River Poetry, Poetry,* and even in *Best American Erotic Poetry.* His book, *Something Wonderful*, is from Redhawk Press, 2021. Another manuscript of his poems crashed on the lunar surface in 2019. Jones was inducted into the NC State Computer Science Hall of Fame in 2021.

Lt Col Melissa Kelley retired from the United States Marine Corps in 2016 after 20 years as a Marine Corps aviator. She was one of the first 5 women Marines to go through Naval Flight Officer training, and one of the first three female aviators in Marine Corps EA-6B Prowler squadrons. Lt Col Kelley's Marine Corps experiences were mostly in line with those of her peers, though occasionally gender did present unique challenges to her service.

An Army dependent, **Anne Kissel** began kindergarten in Germany, finished high school in Hawaii and college in Florida. She worked in elder services and hospice programs in several states and is retired in North Carolina.

Carol Parris Krauss (she, her) is a mother, teacher, and poet from Portsmouth, Virginia. She enjoys using place/nature as theme vehicles. Her poetry can be found at *Dead Mule, Louisiana Literature, Scrawl Place, The Skinny Poetry Journal, Story South, the South Carolina Review, Susurrus, Hastings College Plainsongs, Escape into Life, Bay to Ocean Journal 2021 and 2022,* and Broad*kill Review*. She was honored to be recognized as a Best New Poet by the University of Virginia Press. In 2021, she won the Eastern Shore Writers Association Crossroads Contest and her chapbook, *Just a Spit Down the Road was* published by Kelsay Books. She can be found @CarolKrauss3 (twitter).

Rachel Landsee served in the U.S. Army from 2006-2018 as a paratrooper and lawyer. Her service included two tours in Iraq. In addition to exploring various genres of writing, Rachel chairs a nonprofit organization that promotes new works for the stage and screen. A proud 2021 NEA Veteran Fellow, Rachel lives in Richmond, Virginia with her husband Adam, also an Army veteran, and their children.

Brenda Kay Ledford is a member of North Carolina Writer's Network and listed with "A Directory of American Poets and Fiction Writers." Her work has appeared in many journals including *Our State, Asheville Poetry Review,* and 48 Old Mountain Press Anthologies. Ledford has received the Paul Green Award from NC Society of Historians 13 times for her books and blogs.

Marc Levy served in Vietnam and Cambodia in 1970 as an infantry medic with the First Cavalry Division. His work has appeared in *Litro, Queen's Quarterly, Stand, CounterPunch, New Millennium Writings, The Westchester Review, Fiction International, Collateral, Panorama Travel Journal* and elsewhere. It is forthcoming in *Ragaire Literary Magazine*. He is the author of *How Stevie Nearly Lost the War and Other Postwar Stories*, and has been nominated for a Pushcart Prize. His website is Medic in the Green Time.

Robert Lunday was born at Fort Jackson, South Carolina in 1958 and raised mainly on Army posts in the United States and abroad, including Fort Bragg, North Carolina. In addition to two collections of poetry, *Mad Flights* (Ashland Poetry Press, 2002) and *Gnome* (Black Sun Lit, 2017), he is the author of the memoir *Disequilibria: Meditations on Missingness* (University of New Mexico Press, 2023). He lives in Japan.

Gabriel Maravelas is an Army veteran. During free time, he started writing in a journal. He wrote some poems under the pines to help him process to the outside what was bottled up on the inside. Ever since that experience he has been writing poetry adamantly. It is almost like a form of therapy for him.

Marchiano was born and raised in Brooklyn. He spent a few years putzing around the U.S. working odd-jobs before he decided to be a typical broke millennial and move back to NYC to get an MFA. Marchiano now has an MFA and will soon return to putzing around the U.S. working odd-jobs. Fun fact: Marchiano's also a veteran.

Lenard Duane Moore is a U.S. Army veteran born in 1958, son of a career Marine who served two tours in motor transport with the 5th Communications Battalion in the Republic of Viet Nam. His poems have appeared in print since the early 80s, recently in issues of *North Dakota Quarterly, The Arts Journal,* and *Pembroke Magazine*. He has worked with a variety of societies, organizations, and agencies to promote the arts. His poetry has appeared in translation in Spain, Italy, China, and especially in Japan. His two most recent books are *Long Rain* and *Geography of Jazz*. Moore's brother fought in an artillery unit in Desert Storm.

Andrew Newby is a veteran of the United States Marine Corps and serves as the principal administrator of Veteran & Military Services for the University of Mississippi System. He works to solve the complex issues surrounding military-connected students in higher education, and to get student veterans to, through, and beyond college.

Keith Ockimey is a retired Sergeant E-5 with the United States Army. He has deployed to Bosnia, Honduras, Turkey and Germany during his twenty-three-year term of service.

The United States Marine Corps' **Charles Daniel Perry Jr.**, also artistically known as **CP Maze** has an honesty, identity, and creativity encoded with that of an outlaw; and with his rankings of 3rd & 4th in the World for Performance Poetry speaking for themselves, his stylistics alone he remains crafting. Currently a student in The University of Houston's Creative Writing Poetry program, Maze is determined to leave our world better than we were given it. The Marine Corps ingrained something inside his heart, soul, and work ethic that can't be duplicated. Quoting long-time friend and fellow contemporary Jonathan Brown, "Nothing's impossible, when I'm possible." The Marine Corps and his outlawish craft taught him: Nothings impossible when im/possible.

David W. Plunkett is a Vietnam era veteran, having served in the Coast Guard.

Barbara Presnell a poet, essayist, and non-fiction writer and the daughter and the granddaughter of Purple Heart and Bronze star recipients from the 30th Infantry Division, US Army. Much of her writing for the last ten years has explored both their service and her understanding of how their war experiences shaped them into fathers and citizens. Barbara's book, *Blue Star*, describes their stories and her father's journey across Europe during World War II.

Pat Riviere-Seel is the author of four poetry collections, most recently, *When There Were Horses,* (Main Street Rag, 2021). Her husband, Ed Seel, served as a Special Forces Medic in Vietnam.

Gina Singleton is a mother to 3 kids and a 100% disabled Marine Corps veteran who did two tours in Iraq. As a combat veteran, she served 10 years in the Marine Corps and knows first-hand about dealing with anxiety, depression and memory issues.

Cindy B. Stevens was raised on the East Coast, received a degree in Psychology from Trevecca Nazarene College, and spent her married life in Kentucky and North Carolina. She is the author of *Naked*, a chapbook published by Main Street Rag.

Her poetry has appeared in Pfeiffer University's literary journal, T*he Phoenix*, and in *Heron Clan* anthologies. She enjoys giving public readings and lives in West Hillsborough with her standard poodle, Ruby.

Lee Stockdale has won the United Kingdom National Poetry Prize, the Sidney Lanier Poetry Prize, and other prizes. His work appears in *The Poetry Review, The Guardian, Ekphrastic Review,* anthologies, and elsewhere. His book *Gorilla* was brought out by Main Street Rag Publishing Company in 2022. He enlisted in the Army, stayed for 30 years, and retired as a Judge Advocate Colonel, with stops as a Military Policeman, Infantry Company Commander, and PSYOP Officer. His MFA is from Queens University, Charlotte. He and his wife, a Navy veteran, live in Fairview, NC.

Gina Streaty's poetry and prose have appeared in several online and print publications including *BMa: The Sonia Sanchez Literary Review, Treetops (World Haiku Review), Role Call: A Generational Anthology of Social and Political Black Literature and Art, I've Known Rivers: The (MoAD) Story Project, Martin Luther King Jr: An Anthology of Multicultural Poetry, Obsidian, Hurricane Blues, Solo Café 8&9, TEMBA TUPU! (WALKING NAKED)*, and *South Writ Large*. She has also earned the Zora Neale Hurston Literary Award.

Edward Michael Supranowicz is the grandson of Irish and Russian/Ukrainian immigrants. He grew up on a small farm in Appalachia. He has a grad background in painting and printmaking. Some of his artwork has recently or will soon appear in *Fish Food, Streetlight, Another Chicago Magazine, The Door Is a Jar, The Phoenix,* and *The Harvard Advocate*. Edward is also a published poet.

Ric Vandett served in the USAF from 1962-1966. In the spring of 1963 he was assigned to the US Army and spent two and a half years at Ft. Benning, GA. He went to Vietnam with the First Air Cavalry in September 1965 and was discharged in September 1966.

He was a forward weather observer providing current and forecasted data to helicopter pilots. He is a retired educator. He was a teacher, coach, assistant principal, principal, director, assistant superintendent, and finally superintendent of schools. About 20 years after being discharged, he decided to write about his experiences in Vietnam and began each chapter with an original poem.

For **Daniel Walter**, writing is healing. When he feels at his lowest, he writes. When he is at his highest, he writes. After serving in the Army and deploying multiple times to combat zones, writing became the best therapy for him. Poetry is how he shows his true thoughts

Michael White is a military veteran who served as a communication specialist in Bagdad, Iraq, during the "big surge" in 2006-2007.

Tanya R. Whitney, a retired Army Master Sergeant, served over 27 years with several deployments to Iraq and Afghanistan. She began writing poetry a few years ago as part of her PTSD therapy. Her poetry primarily deals with her military service, but she has also written other pieces. She has had individual poems
and short stories published in several anthologies. She is a 2018 National Veterans Creative Arts Festival Gold Medalist for Creative Writing.

Katherine Wolfe is the daughter of a military vet who fought with the Marines at the Battle of Okinawa in World War II. She states, "He never talked about the war except to say he was on the move a lot and he got malaria on the island. After the war, he still had bouts of chills and fever and was discharged from the service."

Bob Wood served 20 years in the U.S. Air Force and wrote "Father's Hands" on the pages of the aircraft engineer's log while flying missions over the Himalayan Mountains between New Delhi and Tibet. Many years later, he sent those pages to his granddaughter, Shannon Ward, who helped to edit this anthology. He passed away in 2020 at the age of 89.

CREDITS

Selections in this anthology are printed or reprinted with permission from the authors. The following poems, sometimes in different versions, first appeared in the following publications:

Alsop, Maureen. PAPAVER SOMNIFERUM. *Plants Painting Poetry* [video], 2022.

Alsop, Maureen. SWEETWATER ARDOUR. *Sweetwater Ardour* (Yavanika Press), 2022. And *Arbor Vitae* (Nauset Press), 2023.

Balaban, John. "Loving Graham Greene," *Michigan Quarterly Review*, Vol. XLIV, No.1, Winter, 2005.

Balaban, John. "Mr. Giai's Poem." *TriQuarterly*. Spring, 1988.

Balaban, John. "Soldier Home." *The New York Review of Books*. May 26, 2005.

Balaban, John. "Thoughts Before Dawn." *Colorado Review, Vol.* XV, No. 1. 1988.

Barbee, Sam. "Armed Forces." *The Rain We Need*. Press 53. 2016.

Croft, Doug. "Freedom." *Exposed Roots*, 2022.

Hand, Siren. "Birdwatching." *Genesis Literature and Arts Magazine*. 05 January 2021.

Hand, Siren. "Birdwatching." *The After Action Review*. January 2021.

Jackson, Elizabeth. "Soldier, Phoenix." *Poet Lore.* Spring/Summer 2017.

Jones, Paul. "The Jumper." *Something Necessary.* September, 2024. And *Grand Little Things.* November, 2022.

Ledford, Brenda Kay. "Possum Byers." *Leatherwood Falls.* Kelsay Books, 2023.

Levy, Marc. "Casualty Poem." *The Comstock Review.* Fall/Winter 2017.

Lunday, Robert. "Fort Bragg." *Southern Poetry Review.* Spring 1988.

Lunday, Robert. "Fort Bragg." *Mad Flights.* Ashland Poetry Press, 2002.

Moore, Lenard. "A Hum in the Living Room," "Grandmother On the Porch," "My Father Leaves for Vietnam," and "What Was Said on the Porch." *Vietnam Generation Journal,* Vol. 4, No. 3-4. November 1992.

Moore, Lenard. "Vietnam Haiku." *Nobody Gets Off the Bus: The Viet Nam Generation Big Book*, Vol. 5, No. 1-4. March 1994. copyright 1994 by Lenard D. Moore.

Presnell, Barbara. "What Flutters." *Innisfree Poetry Journal.* As part of the collection, *Blu.*

Presnell, Barbara. "Planting the Garden." *Pedestal Magazine.* Issue 82, 2022.

Presnell, Barbara. "Memorial Day, My Son Leaves Home." *Kakalak 2006: An Anthology of Carolina Poetry.* (Press 53), 2016)

Riviere-Seel, Pat. "Firepower" and "Why Pronouns Matter" *When There Were Horses.* 2021.

Stockdale, Lee. "Battlefield." *Gorilla.* Main Street Rag Publishing Company. 2022.

Whitney, Tanya R. "Only a Dream." *The Cuddy Family Foundation for Veterans Poetry Journal,* Vol. 5, March 2023.

Wolfe, Katherine "My Father's Gift." *Hermit Feathers Review.* 2022.